# MY TRAVEL MEMOIRS

# MY TRAVEL MEMOIRS

## PART ONE:
## BANGLADESH, JORDAN, AND EUROPE

### ANIMESH RAY

PARTRIDGE

**To order additional copies of this book, contact**
Partridge India
000 800 10062 62
orders.india@partridgepublishing.com

www.partridgepublishing.com/india

# Dedicated to my father
## COL (Dr) Anil Chandra Ray (Retired)
## On his 100th Birthday

(8th of May 1912 to 14th of December 2012)

My father, Colonel (Retd) Anil Chandra Ray was born in a humble home in a village of East Bengal (now in Bangladesh). His father, Akshay Chandra Ray, was a just, honest and a persevering man who had bound his family with the bondage of love, honesty, simplicity and discipline. He had not studied beyond high school and was a *Patwari* (a person responsible to keep a record of land distribution and collect land revenue from the land owners and deposit that money in the government treasury) He had fathered a brood of ten siblings, seven of them girls and three boys. In those days getting a girl married was in itself a daunting task. Anil was his eldest son, dearly loved by his parents and rest of the family. He was destined to face many challenges from his early childhood days. Very early in his life, his ancestral home, which in those days used to be of wooden construction, beautiful though, was burnt to ashes due to a devastating fire in his village. Anil enjoyed his studies. To continue his education at the tender age of six, he had to move from village to village, compromising with all forms of difficulties to ensue an admission in a good school. Therefore he had to staying with distant relatives, far away from his own home, so his education would not suffer.

One out of many stringent customs those days was for parents to get their brood married as early as possible. In August 1933, at the tender age of twenty, when he was barely a man, Anil was married to Chitralekha, a petite lass of fourteen from a nearby village. Marriage ceremony was celebrated with the customary pomp and soon after, Anil had to leaving his young wife at his ancestral home at village Potazia, District Pabna, East Bengal to take care of his parents and their growing children, who were not yet married. Without any thought of a honeymoon, Anil had to immediately move to Calcutta for a six year long course in medicine, at the coveted Calcutta

Medical College. On graduating as a fully qualified medical doctor, that is after completion of one year of house surgeon job in a hospital, in the month of March1940, Anil was commissioned into the Royal Indian Medical Corps, as a doctor and posted to Rawalpindi.

He stay at Rawalpindi, India was very short, as he along with his small medical unit was shipped to Iraq to join the British troops already assembled there for rigorous desert warfare training. Hitler had planned his North African Campaign well, with an eye on the oil fields of the Middle East. So, for the next three years Anil's war experience was plentiful. He had moved from Iraq to Syria, then Aden to Alexandria, thereafter to the beautiful island of Sicily and finally moved through the battle ravaged Italy to its North. The war was not over yet for budding Anil. He was shipped back to India. After a brief holiday with his family he moved to the Indo-Burma border for more warlike activities in the insects infested and malaria ridden jungles of Burma. Thus, my father along with the British Indian troops, along with other allied forces was heavily engaged in hurricane like war activities in the deserts of North Africa and the jungles of Burma. Anil as a sincere medical officer had many other responsibilities, which included patiently listening and consoling the traumas and wounds of the battle ravaged soldiers, who came to him for treatment.

My father Anil was indeed a worthy son of India. In his prime days, he was totally engrossed in practicing medicine and has been declared as one of the pioneering neurosurgeons of our independent India. As an soldier of Indian Army he has served nobly for over 30 years. And during WW II he had to faced the wrath of Nazi Germany and vengeance of the Japanese Army. He has been a prolific reader of Vedic literature and expressed theological reasoning of some of the difficult Vedic slokas, which have been appreciated by many learned scholars. He is blessed with two sons and a daughter, with names respectively as Animesh, Ashish and Pronoti. Even to this day, he stands erect and keeps abreast with all that is happening around him.

By Animesh Ray

Animesh Ray

# A PRELUDE BY THE AUTHOR

After retiring from the army in 1991, and completion of as many of our commitments, I along with my wife Swapna, have been travelling to many of the exotic places we were keen to see. Many years later, after our trip to Europe in 2010, I felt an urge to write a Travel Memoir from my scrap notes and picture albums dearly held in my possession. My was keen that I publish some of my experiences which he felt will certainly be enjoyed by a reader. After some years I decided to pen my thoughts. While penning my thoughts my mind was constantly floating back to my childhood days in North Bengal. I was born in that part of Bengal which is now Bangladesh. Most of my formative years were spent in that part of the world till I was 11 years of age. I stayed there during the Indo–Pak partition of August 1947. I was finally sent from East Pakistan to India in the month of August 1948, to join my parents in India at Pune. After my graduation, I joined the Indian Army. Surprisingly, twenty three years after leaving East Pakistan, in April

1971 I was fighting side by side with the Bangladesh Muktibahinr over the next nine months, in their battle of independence against the Armed forces of Pakistan. Finally, my thoughts moved to our first visit to Europe in 2010, when we visited Jordon, Italy, Austria, onward to the Principality of Liechtenstein, Switzerland, Germany, Netherland, France and finally reached the shores of United Kingdom of Britain. I remember reaching London only a day before the marriage of Prince William of Wales to Kate, who was a commoner from Wales. Their marriage was solemnized on 29th of April 2011.

In this book of mine I have dared to pen some of my first impressions of the people of Bangladesh, Jordon and Europe and their sense of dignity, pride, confidence and general approach to life. I could see the spark in the eyes of the people, while they narrated the tales of their agonizing past and talked of the ways they had survived the onslaughts of their invaders, who had mercilessly raped their motherland in centuries past. In spite of the many obstacles faced by the common people, they had wishfully withstood many hardships, finally to grow from strength to strength and be in a position to reclaim much of what was lost to their forefathers. In my opinion those are some of the character qualities that have finally bound people together to a progressively thinking nation which can last for many centuries in spite of many upheavals faced by them, they were standing strongly united. Meer slogans and the burning of government properties can ever give justice to people, and obviously, can never build a truly independent nation.

Initially I thought of sharing my travel experiences only with the younger generations of my family and friends. As I progressed with written this Travel Memoir, I decided to share my book with any and everyone who enjoy reading travel experiences of others to decide on the places to visit in near future. I tried to understand the historic background of each one of the places I travelled. And tried to learn about them. Their way of living in the present world and many more thing about the places I had travelled to. This book may also interest those who, for some reason or the other are unable to travel to many of the exotic places of this beautiful world and see for themselves the virtues that lie within. Many books and movies and TV serials are available, but to my mind a video session alone or a random talk on a subject cannot replace a small book containing valuable information about a place. When travelling to a new place for the first time, we desire to know more about that place, the people, their culture, customs and the places to visit and the things to do and many more things to carry home. There are ample references material available in different books or on exhaustive studies on any specific aspects of study. Somewhere, during the process of penning my thoughts I felt the need to present my travel notes to those who consider taking a plunge into travelling to see and judge for themselves the new and exciting places the world has to offer, but are still hunting for many useful information or reading material of the places of their interest. The idea is to provide as much information about a place in this small book and leave the matters for a deeper plunge into the subject or place from deeper studies or a research. My travel memoirs perhaps may also interest those intending to refresh their memories of their past visits to some of the places I have mentioned or merely to glance through this book as a coffee table material.

My many thanks to my friends, relatives and my local tour guides who patiently answered many of my queries, and also interacted with the locals to give me many useful information about the land and people that are dwelling there. My special thanks to my dear wife for bearing with me as I used to burnt the midnight oil in search of some valued information. I take this opportunity to thank Mrs.Sandhaya Sinha. She had shared with me her opinion on a large number issues and was kind enough to pen her valued opinion on this book. This Travel Memoirs may be of some help to those who wish to travel to places without the help of a formal guide.

Animesh Ray

# MY TRAVEL MEMOIRS

## PART – 1
### (BANGLADESH, JORDAN, ITALY, AUSTRIA, PRINCIPILITY OF LIECHTENSTEIN, SWITZERLAND, GERMANY, BELGIUM, FRANCE AND UNITED KINGDOME)

BY ANIMESH RAY

# BANGLADESH

$W$hy would anybody want to travel to Bangladesh? Do people travel to a place purely for pleasure? What is there to see in Bangladesh? These are some of the questions that haunt many of us before deciding a trip to any place. Prior to the narration of my personal glimpses of Bangladesh, I thought it proper to reflect on the history of this country that was once a part of India. At the very start I must add caution that we, the people who are the natives of this parts of the world were never good at maintain honest records, or have had the dignity to preserve the relics of our predecessors. Even then there exist stupendous things on this vast land to see and learn from. On account of certain religious sentiments, a very few of us, individually or collectively picked up a sword to defend what was rightfully our own. Even then, over the time there have been many great philosophers and dynamic rulers in the Bihar- Bengal region between 560 BC and 180 BC like Siddhartha Gautama (the Buddha), the Magadha empire, which included rulers like Chandragupta Maurya, Bindusara, Vikramaditya, Asoka and a few were from this part of the world. But their achievements have not been properly recorded. Some of their achievements and living conditions prevailing then had come down to us through the unbiased records maintained by the foreign travelers and scholars like Fa Hein to this land.

In the ancient times, Bengal region was an active part of the formidable Hindu Empire. With passage of time, the Hindu empire, mainly from Magadha in east had stretched its hegemony across the length and breadth of India and without bloodshed, had spread Hinduism across the entire South East Asia and Buddhism had spread across Tibet and China to Korea and Japan. Whereas history is replete with incidence of conquerors carried away the goodies of the occupied land for the prosperity of their own country or for their personal use, leaving the chumps for the vanquished. There have been instances where the conquerors have massacred the aborigines of the occupied land and settled the people of their land to start a new life and to rule over the people of the occupied land. This had happened in almost every part of the world. Similarly, the colonial powers prospered by importing raw materials at very cheap rates from the occupied land and exported the finished products back to the same region at a much high costs.

The WWII ended on 31 December 1945, giving birth to a new world order with the advent of the United Nation. The colonial rulers of Europe began giving independence to many of their third world countries. Thus the present generation began living peacefully as in a world community. And yet the exploitation by the developed nations continued through their commercial practices of import of raw materials from the developing countries at a low rate and exports the finished products back to them at exorbitant rates. Some of the newly independent nations, apart from having to deal with untrained manpower at every echelon of nation building, are finding extreme difficulties in controlling rampant corruption by the political parties and many others, resulting in a slower rate of national developments and dissatisfaction by the ruling mass. But, most of these developing countries have attracted tourists from world over; Bangladesh is one of such destinations.

To understand the history of the People's Republic of Bangladesh commenced on 26 March 1971 when the people of Bangladesh declared their independence from Pakistan. Bangladesh celebrates Victory Day on 16 December 1971 when the Bangladesh Mukti Bahini along with Mitro Bahini that is Indian Armed Forces liberated Bangladesh from Pakistan. The present day Bangladesh was once a seafaring people following Hindu region like the people of the rest of Hindustan. Between 16th and mid 18th centuries the Afghans and the Moguls ruled over this part of Hindustan had been forcefully or by inducement, converting the natives to follow the Muslim faith. The Dutch, French and the British had established separate East India trading companies in this region in the 16th to 18th centuries. On 23 December 1757, the British East India Company under Robert Clive defeated Nawab Siraj-ud-daulah at the Battle of Palassey in Bengal. In 1772 Warren Hastings was appointed the Governor of Bengal. The British Crown had ruled over East Bengal, now Bangladesh till 14 August 1947, when the British finally left the Union of India.

# The Glories Ancient Bengal

To trace the history of Bangladesh one needs to take a plunge into the pre-historic period of Bengal when the Vanga Kingdom was a powerful seafaring nation of Ancient India. Moving around to other parts like the South East Asia one feels convinced about the presence of Bengali people in those regions. I those days they had overseas trade relations with Java, Sumatra and Siam (modern day Thailand). According to Mahavamsa (a historic poem written in the Pali language of the kings of Sri Lanka), the Vanga prince Vijaya Singha conquerwd Lanka (modern Sri Lanka) in 544 BC and gave the name "Sinhala" to the country. The seafaring Bengali people migrated to the maritime Southeast Asia and established their own colony there.

The pre-Gupta period of Bengal is shrouded with obscurity. Before the conquest of Samudragupta, Bengal was divided into two kingdoms, Pushkarana and Somatota. Chandragupta II had defeated a confederacy of Vanga kings resulting in Bengal becoming part of Gupta Empire.

By the 6th century, the Gupta Empire ruled over the northern Indian subcontinent was largely broken up. East Bengal became the Vanga Kingdom while the Ganda Kingdom rose in the west with their capital at Karnasavarna (Murshidabad). Shashanka, a vessal of the last Gupta Empire became independent and unified the smaller principalities of Bengal (Gour, Vanga, and Samatala) and vied for regional power with Harshavardana in north India. But this burst of Bengal power did not last beyond his death as Bengal descended afterward into a period marked by disunity and frequent invasion. The development of Bengal calendar is also attributed to Shahanka as the statuary date falls squarely within his reign (600 AD – 625 AD).

The next thrust forward of Bengal was during the Pala dynasty which was the first independent Buddhist dynasty of Bengal. The name Pala (in Bengal pal) means protector and was used as an ending to the names of all Pala monarchs. The Pala was followed by the Mahayana and Trantic school of Buddhism. Gopala was the first ruler from the dynasty. This event is recognized as one of the first democratic election in South Asia. The Buddhist dynasty lasted for four centuries (750 AD – 1120 AD) and shared its period of stability and prosperity in Bengal. They created many temples and work of art as well as supported the University of Nalanda and Vikramashila. Somapura Mahavihara built by Dharmapala, now in Bangladesh is the greatest Buddhist Vihara in the Indian subcontinent. The Palas were responsible for the introduction of Mahayana Buddhism in Tibet, Bhutan and Mayanmar. The Palas had extensive trade as well as influence in the south-east Asia. This period can be called the Golden period in the history of Bengal. Which can be seen in the sculptures and architectural style of the Sailendra Empire (present-day Malaya, Java, and Sumatra)?

The Palas were followed by the Sena dynasty that brought under one rule during the 12th century. Vijay Sen the second ruler of this dynasty defeated the last Pala emperor Madnapala and established his reign. Ballal Sena introduced caste system in Bengal and made Nabadwip the capital. The fourth king of this dynasty Lakshman Sen expanded the beyond Bengal to Bihar. Later Lakshman fled to eastern Bengal under the onslaught of the Muslims without facing him in battle.

## Pakistan –The Bangladesh problem

India and Pakistan gained Dominion Status when the British India was divided to form the Socialist Republic of India and Islamic Pakistan in August 1947. Mohammed Jinna formed the Islamic Pakistan with its two wings comprising the Muslim dominated eastern half of Bengal province to form East Pakistan, separated by 1600 km Indian territory was West Pakistan, which comprising the province of Sindh, west portion of the province of Punjab and the vastly tribal regions of Makran, Kharan and the north-western provinces of Bhaluchistan, Quetta and Peshwar. The east wing of Pakistan shared a common Bengali language and were socially united, whereas the western wing of Pakistan was burdened with a large number of hardy mountain tribes practicing Muslim religion but spoken different tribal dialects, whereas the people of the Sindh region spoke Sindhi language and the people of Punjab communicated in Punjabi. Islamic religion and Urdu language was made the official national language of Pakistan, which was mainly spoken by the educated Muslims.

For almost nine years after Independence, Pakistan remained a dominion territory. It proclaimed to be an Islamic republic on 23 March 1956. Field

Martial Ayub Khan seized power in 1958 and ruled until March 1969 when he was deposed by General Yahya Khan. In the first free elections in December 1970 Sheikh Mujibur Rahman's Awami League swept the board in the East, whereas Zulfikar Ali Bhutto of Pakistan People's Party with a much lesser margin of votes won in the western wing. General Yahya Khan did not wish to handover the reign of Pakistan to Sheikh Mujibur Rahimon. A peacefully civil protest led by the Bengali speaking population of East Pakistan was crushed by the West Pakistani dominated military troops stationed in East Pakistan. Sheikh Mujibur Rahman was arrested in March 1971 from East Pakistan and dispatched to an unknown destination in West Pakistan. The entire Bengali population staged an uprising. Which was savagely crushed and merciless killing, rape and plunder was being carried out by the West Pakistani troops assisted by the pro West Pakistani Muslim population who had migrated to East Pakistan during the partition of India and Pakistan in 1947.

## Glimpses of British India and Bangladesh

Surprisingly I was born in a remote village called Potazia in district Pabna of Purbo Bangla (now in Bangladesh), and lived there with my Grandparents till I was 11 years of age. My father was commissioned into British Indian Army in1940 and very soon moved to Iraq, Syria, North Africa, Malta, Italy and Indo-Burma border till the end of the world war in September 1945.

In 1946 the British Indian Army was being demobilized to half its war-time strength. Simultaneously the British troops and other allied forced of Australia, Africa and the USA, stationed in India was leaving this country, which caused multifaceted administrative strains on the civil and military administration of then British India.

During the latter stage of India's struggle for freedom from the British, in and around 1940, the seeds of racial discontent were sown in the minds of a few self-seeking Hindu and Muslim leaders who were seeking self-rule in India. Soon, after the Second World War was over, in August 1947, British-India was divided into two independent states of India and Pakistan. Same year, during the partition of India, more than one third of the remaining

British Indian armed forces and civil administrative service personnel, who had opted to be a part of new India or Pakistan, was swap over to their new motherlands. It was decided that Pakistan would be the homeland for all Muslim people only, including those Muslims from Hindu India, who wished to move to Islamic Pakistan. India was to be the home for all those people, irrespective of cast, creed or religion who wished to live in India, which included those Hindus and the people of other religious faith who wished to make India their permanent home. This political decision, caused confusion and disharmony, and lead to communal disharmony between the Hindus and Muslims. The same people who had lived peacefully for centuries after the death of the Moghul Emperor Aurangzeb. Those very people of the Indian subcontinent, had lived in harmony before the idea of two nation theory was injected into them. Improper execution of the two nation formula for India and Pakistan had put the newly born countries in the grip of communal riots; finally escalated into a grim genocide of innocent people. Massacre of Hindus by the Muslims, and in retaliation the masseur of Muslims by the Hindus. The entire country was in turmoil. Overnight, the people who were friends became enemies. Rape, plunder and destruction caused as a result of the partition of India to give the Muslims an exclusive piece of land to live in was the slogan. Thus, a country named Pakistan was carved out of the Hindu dominated India. As the days of the partition approached, rumors spread. Overnight, began the exchange of large contingence of people along with their little money, food and other belongings in whatever mode of transportation they could gather, the people were moving from India to Pakistan. Similarly the ill-fated people were on exodus from Pakistan to Indian, and thereafter they were put into concentration camps, staggered on both sides of the newly formed borders between India and Pakistan, in search of a new home, a place to stay in any part of new India. The civil administration was in turmoil. On both sides, their armed forces were well trained under the British and were quickly rushed to play a major role towards quelling the communal disturbances, and to maintain law-and-order in both parts of the newly independent states of India and Pakistan. Both these countries were gripped in the midst of the most violent communal riots the modern world has ever witnessed. As the reshuffling of troops was in process, the depleted strength on the Indian and the new Pakistani Armed Forces had to face the brunt of the communal turmoil. They were able to bring about normalcy in their respective countries, as the bulk of the British officials deputed to the Indian Civil Services along with the British officers of Indian Armed Forces were simultaneously leaving India and Pakistan, whereas both the newly independent country was in flames. In those days I was a little boy, barely 10 years old and saw all that was happening with my own eyes.

All these stimulating activities, coupled with the long drawn military operations to repel the Pakistani invasion of Kashmir commenced in 1948 had left a deep impression in my mind. My father, as an Indian Army officer was constantly on the move. All these factors grossly affected my schooling but I was still in East Pakistan (now Bangladesh). In September 1948, my Grandfather finally allowed me to go to India, to join my father who was then posted at Pune in Maharastra in those days. In my early days in India I had travelled to many parts of the country on account of the frequent posting of my father in India and abroad. My aim of this narration is to tell the readers about the destabilization caused the people of the country due to the partition of India.

My travelling days continued. A decade later, as a Major in the Indian Army, I was commanding a battery of guns in the foot-hills of Assam near Bhutan. On the 10th of April 1971, while I was in the midst of a routine military exercise, I was ordered back to my main location to find my troops in combat readiness, with guns, ammunition and all warlike provisions and logistic supports. All lineups to move with me, in a military convoy of my unit vehicles, to an unknown destination, for an indefinite period of time, somewhere along the Indo-Pak border near the town of Tura in Meghalaya. We reached our destination after a day and night long journey. I was given a formal welcome to the K sector of military operation, and quickly briefed by the Sector Commander, Brigadier Sant Singh. He looked tired but patiently narrated the grim situation across the border. I was to take stock of the military operational aspect of the sector. I was permitted to move my batter of guns at my discretion and provide artillery fire support to the numerous Indian border outposts manned by the scantily equipped battalion of BSF (Border Security Force) troops deployed in far-flung sections and platoons post stretched along the Indo-Pak border of the Garo Hills in Meghalaya. My task was to provide artillery fire support all along the 200 km long border with Pakistan, stretched in semi-hilly terrain between Baghmara in the east to Mankachar in the west facing the mighty River Brahmaputra. In due course my task also included providing technical advice and artillery support to the military operations being launched across the border by the Muktibahini forces under the command of then Brigadier Ziaul Rahiman, who as a Bengali officer of Pakistan Army, with valor had courageously revolted against the Pakistani regime. He, along with many of the Bengali officers and soldiers had crossed over to India territory forcible support. At the time of his mutiny Ziaul Rahiman was a superseded Majors of a Pakistani infantry officer, posted as the Second-in-command of a Bengali Infantry Battalion of the Pakistan Army. This audacious officer had revolted, by imprisoning his West Pakistani Commanding Officer. He, along with the revolting Bengali soldiers, capturing a radio station, and over the radio in East Pakistan broadcasted the Independence of Bangladesh... Subsequently, he along with his dedicated troops fled to Tripura in India, from there, he along with his troops moved to Tura in India in order to regroup, refit and recruit the young, old, as well the politically motivated Bengali Muslims, who were swarming across to the Indian territory for their day to day provisions, shelters and every other possible support from Indian government till the liberation of Bangladesh.

Ziaul Rahiman's immediate goal was to garner maximum support to launch military attacks across the Indian border with help from India to dismember as many of the West Pakistani troops positioned in Bangladesh. In the mean while the Pakistani troops ruthlessly massacred the helpless Bengali population under their control. The Pakistani army along with their supporters raped the women and raised their property to the ground or took possession of the property to be given to the Bihar Muslims who had crossed over to East Bengal during the Indo-Pak partition in 1947, and were the supporters to the West Pakistani cause. Many of these Bihar Muslims were recruited as Razakars. They were conducting loot, gruesome murders, rapes, torture and destruction or forceful occupation of the properties belonging to the Bengali speaking people, as they were forced to flee from their home due to the genocide...

After the independence of Bangladesh in December 1971, the country was once again in turmoil due to the economic recessions caused by drying up of funds and resources by the West Pakistani financiers. In the turmoil that followed were the politically motivated Bangladeshis. Ultimately they plotted a Military takeover of the recently formed state of Bangladesh. Shaik Mujebur Rehman was assassinated by the loyal troops of Ziaul Rahman, who himself become the next President of Bangladesh. Later he too, was assassinated by his fellow soldiers, in order to make Genera Ershad their next president.

While commanding my troops in Meghalaya in April 1970, I was deputed to be the artillery adviser to Ziaul Rahiman till October 71. I was required to participate in many of the attacks launched by the Mukti Bahini under Ziaul Rahiman across the Indo-Pak border into the Pakistani occupied positions. This involved moving deeper inside the Pakistan territory to identify and register military targets which were well inside the Mymensingh district of East Pakistan. Thereafter, I along with my battery move to the Begonia bulge in Tripura, India, to join my regular army troops in the battles of Belonia, on to Laksham, Chandpur, Mainamoti, Fenny and finally to reach Chittagongin January 1972 and remained there for a few months after the liberation of Bangladesh.

## Topography of Bangladesh

As I have mentioned earlier my grand-parents refused to accompany me to India as they were deeply in love with the lush green fields of his motherland Bengal. He had fallen in love with the people of Pubro Bangla. The hamlet at Potazia where we lived was called "Raipara". This part of the world is at the confluence of the mighty River Jamuna (Brahmaputra) and River Ganga (Ganges) of the undivided India. The entire region is bound within the delta of the two voluminous rivers and their tributaries. So the region is a low-lying delta created over many thousands of years of erosion by the mighty force of rivers creating a large stretch of fertile agricultural land. Large areas were dug in the past centuries to build mounds to live on and the low line areas became the water reservoirs in the dry seasons and totally submerged during the rainy seasons. If one cared to go on a stroll on any one of those patches of land sticking out of the large stretches of the island in any direction he would soon have reached the other end of that island. There were chains of thousands of such chains of small or bigger islands stretching out as though onto the sea. Some of the interesting features of this part of the world I have narrated below.

After the rainy season, that is mid-autumn to mid-spring majority of the streams and the man-made water channels connecting the many water reservoirs around the high grounds would be drying up. The only mode of transportation for long distances in those seasons was by primitive looking carts having bamboo flooring, fixed on a wooden block running breath wise through the centre of the cart. The central block of wood working as an axle suspended by a pair of wooden wheels attached on either side. One can easily distinguish these oxen-carts carrying people of status as those would have an arched covering of bamboo mashing to provide protection to the travelers from dust, rain or sunshine. This vehicle has no shock observers and is pulled by a pair of healthy bulls. The vehicle jerked while moving and bounced while negotiating roughs on the cart-tracks on the muddy soils of "Sonar Bangla", meaning Golden Bengal. While moving this cart would churn up whatever was inside ones stomach. So, it would be wise not to travel after a heavy meal. During the better part of spring to autumn season, one would see the harvesting of the golden rice crops or notice silvery-golden dust swirling in the distance sky. Maybe you notice farmers merrily sloughing their fields for the next crop. Occasionally, one would come across stretches of green fields nurturing the short-stem variety of paddy. Other green fields may be of mustard or luscious sapling of sweet-pea swaying with the flow of the easterly winds. One would perhaps see many bullock-carts laden with sacks full of recently harvested grain stacked and moved in a bullock-cart convoy to granaries of a Zamindar (Land owner). The cranky wooden wheels of the carts ploughed up dust as the convoy rattled down the slopes of the dry river beds; finally to climb up the far banks of the meandering dry river-bed. This very river, that was not very long ago furious in spates, roaring like a loin and flooding its banks. To travel longer distances people still move in bullock-carts to reach a memorable road-head or to reach a ferry point, from where further travel would either be by an overloaded truck, bus or larger river-crafts with sales. Thereafter, the move was again, by bus or bullock-cart till reaching ones destination or a railway station. To travel 20 to 25 miles, one would take anywhere up to 8 to 10 hours.

In my childhood days as I occasionally travelled with my mother or grand-father to meet relatives in other villages or towns in the region I would see stretches of open space interspersed by clusters of houses neatly spaced with mango groves, lines after lines of cocoanut palm or boatel palm. At places one can see clusters of banana plants or bamboo groves. This was the land of many a pristine beauty.

Even in 1971, during my travels across the length and breadth of this country with the Muktibahini and later when the Indian troops had crossed over the border, I realized that the local people of Bangladesh were still as simple and innocent as they were a couple of decades earlier when I lived in that country. I remembered seeing those hardy people; regardless of consequences painstakingly find the remedies to the hazards caused by the unpredictable climatic challenges. They were peace loving people, innocent and followed pristine values and love their folk-music and "Bhatiyali" songs. The intellectual lot recites Tagore and sang Rabindrasangeets or Nazroolgeets. Unfortunately, majority of the people were not very well-read and totally unaware of the advancements made in other parts of the world. After the Hindus left for India, more than 80 percent of the remaining population was the converted Muslims from the lower casts of Hindus during the 400 years of Muslim rule. During the British rule the Muslims comprised the major portion of the work-force of this amicably blended Hindu-Muslim society. But now, more than two decades after the partition, except for a spurt of formal education there was hardly any material progress made by the Bengali Muslims of East Pakistan. They continued to live in their primitive ways. As in the past, the landless Bengali Muslims plough the fields for their West Pakistani or Bihar Muslim masters. As a living they still rear livestock for milk and meat, fish in plenty from the rivers, streams and numerous water tanks, chicken and eggs in plenty and enjoy fresh vegetables from their little kitchen-gardens. They are good fishermen and habituated to rowing boats and singing their melodious Bhatiyali folksongs. Before the partition about 3o to 40 percent of the population were Bengali Hindus: some of them left during Indo-Pak partition in 1947, but the remaining gradually left their property behind under threats incited by the West Pakistani regime or during the uprising in Noakhali and Dhaka stimulated because of Jinnah's two-nation-theory which was being sponsored by the Muslim League. British regime generally encouraged harmony between the Hindus and Muslims so they freely attend each other's religious functions. The people in general merrily followed unique

Hindu-Muslim cultural patterns and attended each other's marriages and festivals. The British rulers who travelled to these regions were few and far between, they were generally the higher executives who would occasionally pay symbolic visits to their district in order to ensure that the local lords were loyal to the British crown, regularly paid the revenues, as well to ensure stability in the region through a strong and loyal police force.

I carry vivid memories of the monsoons in East Bengal (now Bangladesh). The long stemmed paddy and jute are primarily cultivation in this part of the world. The peculiarity of this variety of paddy sapling is that it grows taller with the swelling of water in the fields under cultivation. The rains and the melting snow from the Himalayan peaks in the north would gradually submerge a large portion of this region. In the summer months, particularly due to heavy monsoon rains, the water level would rise by 10ft to 14ft above the ground level. As the rivers swelled and flooded a large portion of the land-mass leaving clusters of high ground above the water-line. The financially prosperous people, living in permanent brick houses. They would build temporary shelters for their livestock and temporary thatch huts for the marooned farm-hands/ tillers of the landlords land as a shelter for living during the rainy seasons. During the monsoons when most of the landmass is inundated, a movement between the chains of high-grounds was by small boats or bamboo-rafts. Larger boats, steamers and trawlers would be used on the main rivers. The larger rivers would invariably be very turbulent during the frequent storms or cyclones, causing massive destruction to the growing paddy crop and all that come in its way. Yet, the place is amazingly beautiful to look at; the people are simple, sincere, hardworking and God fearing. It is here, the poet laureate Rabindranath Tagore would come on his frequent vests to rest and to write some of his literary masterpieces. I was told that the song, "Sonar Bangla" (Golden Bengal), the National Anthem of Bangladesh was written by Tagore, while he was on one of his visit to this part of Bengal,

Paradoxically, as a soldier in those eight eventful months my stay in East Pakistan, now Bangladesh I had to pump tons and tons of rockets bombs and artillery shells in some of those very regions where I had loved to stay in my childhood day. But my flare for travelling to exotic places continues to this day.

# MY LAST TRIP ABROAD

In mid April this year (2011) during the spring season, when flowers bloom at their best, birds merrily chirp and a general atmosphere of gaiety prevails, I, along with my dear wife, proceeded on a month's trip to Europe. One may say this trip was one of our many second honeymoons we spent and yet we don't seem to understand each other.

Our tour of Europe commenced and ended at Delhi. The trail blazing path commenced with a short halt at Amman in Jordon, from where we took a flight to Rome. Thereafter we moved by a luxury bus through the center of the European mainland. The route specifically covered a large portion of the ancient Roman Empire moving northward through the centre of Europe, finally to reach London in about 15 days.

Our last holidaying trip abroad was about five years ago to South East Asia. That was well before my mother had expired. Out tour of Europe commence on the 16<sup>th</sup> of April 2011. Our last few days at Lucknow before the trip was for minute tie-ups, interspersed with mirth and exuberance, particularly because we were ultimately going to meet my younger son Abhijit and his family in England. My son Arijit had meticulously arranged for our short stay at Gurgaon. Having enjoyed a full day rest at Gurgaon, early in the morning the sky was still ash-grey, we moved to Delhi International airport for our journey by a Royal Jordanian Airways flight to Amman.

# JORDON

## Amman

Air-travel from Delhi to Amman had to be hurriedly rescheduled. I recall someone had remarked that the women of Jordon were naive, but men were exceedingly capricious. During my return trip's 24 hours transit stay at Amman I realized how true this statement was. Many from our touring group complained about their luggage been tampered with and valuables removed. The prompt replies by the airport staff were we have to carry out intensive security checks. Have to do the same thing even in the cargo room on every transit halts and again before reloading of the cargoes in to aircrafts. Our complaints never got a satisfying reply from the airport authorities, except for a hint on the troubles brewing in the Middle-East. As we commenced our journey from Delhi, the political turmoil caused by the uprisings against the corrupt government in Egypt was gradually trickling into the mindset of the restless people of Libya being ruled by another dictator Gaddafi. The turmoil caused had spilled further to the rest of Arab world. But Jordan though a Muslim nation remains peaceful. Our tour provider had to make many last minute changes to our air travel. Apprehensively, the two of us boarded the Royal Jordan Airways flight with an offer of a sightseeing halt at Amman. I was reticent to tell my wife all the possible dangers because of the nearness of trouble hit Syria, Palestine and other volatile Muslim states to Jordan. During our brief stay at Amman, we saw a large influx of Muslim passengers streaming out of the airport, and while boarding the plane at Amman for Rome I noticed my wife was hesitant and was sitting at the edge of her seat. She cast a questioning look. I concluded, maybe due to the political disturbances in the Middle East many have cancelled their trip.

Food and services on board the Royal Jordanian airline were excellent. What struck me most were the smart, confident yet innocent, good looks of the air- hostesses. I was certain they were Arabs with a sting somewhere of Greek features. I remembered then that since ancient times Jordan was a bustling trading centre between West Asia, Africa and Mediterranean Europe. History is replete with tales of David and later Solomon who had incorporated parts of present-day Jordan into their kingdoms. Times thereafter, the religious cults of the Romans, Jews, Christians, Arabs and the Byzantine Empire have held sway on this arid land. From the 16th century till 1918, Jordan was a part of the Turkish Ottoman Empire. The land still is desolated barren desert, thinly populated with nomadic tribes settled in clusters of clay huts and scattered date palm, the cities are well maintained thriving with an air of modernity.

## Modern History of Jordan

In 1920, the area comprising Transjordan, as it was then called, became a part of the British mandate of Palestine. In 1927, Transjordan became an independent state under the British mandate. In 1949, Jordan annexed the West Bank territory. Britain had taken a fancy to Jordan so it remained under the British Empire till Jordan was granted independence after the WWII. Unlike other neighboring states, the King of Jordan adopted a democratically elected constitutional monarchy. With the passage of time, in spite of its autonomous ruler, the people of Jordan have been accepting outside interferences till ages. Ask the community! With increased social freedom and better education, the common people are now demanding further constituent changes in their governance by the King. The population is predominantly Muslim, with wide socio-economic gaps. Palestine gained independence with unsolved issues between the Arabs and the Jews. Jordan continues to remain a barren desert land popularly known for date fruits, ancient caves and phosphorous. Tourism flourished due to the world famous Dead Sea and the ancient cave relics at Patra. Yet it enjoys far better per-capita-income than of India.

# EUROPE

## ITALY

### Rome

#### Ancient Roman Empire

On reaching Rome our Tour Manager met us at the airport, he introduced himself as Amit Kulkarni and quickly corrected himself, call me Amit. I was soon impressed by his smart looks and affable nature. He escorted us to a hallway at the airport where, for the first time, we met the rest of our tour team. After a brief introducing each one of our 47 tour members, we commenced our 'European Grand Tour' by boarding the luxury bus owned and driven by Mario, an Italian.

The bus slowly meandered around the historic Seven Hills of Rome. Each one of these hills had a story to tell, of a dynasty, a kingdom, a period etched in the history of Rome, Italy, Europe or for that matter affecting the history of the world at large. As we moved I developed sympathy for the common people of the land for their tolerance to the harsh changes imposed by their foreign rulers and which lasted through the rise and fall of the Vikings, Greeks, Egyptians, Barbarians and in particular the 12 centuries of rigid rule by the Roman lords. The people of the land still continued to display a bond of solidarity within their community. We moved on, Amit narrated the tales of the Seven Hills. I was astounded and listened carefully as he flawlessly narrated the dignifying details of the history of Rome. Finally, at 6 PM we walked into a shanty Indian restaurant for dinner. Some of our members objected to an early dinner, the shabby arrangements and frugal food items laid out for us to eat. Most of us did not enjoy the meal. We complained to Amit, and our subsequent meals had the necessary quantity, quality and decor. However, there is a point which many of us tourists were not aware of, and that is in Europe, for six months commencing in spring, days are much longer than the nights and light suppers are taken when the sun is still visible.

## The 3D-rewind of Ancient Roman Empire

After supper, we were given a short but amusing talk on the history of the Roman Empire by a professional guide. He told us the purpose of building the Coliseum. He emphatically narrated that the true story is not what the English movie thrillers depict. The Coliseum was primarily designed as a common place for the multiple ways to entertain the people of Rome and their lords. He shared with us the long history of Rome. Then we moved through time to the 3D Rewind of ancient Rome, it was like taking our place in history. We experienced an exhilarating three dimensional journey through the history of imperial Rome. Thanks to a series of spectacular unique effects we found ourselves back in the first century ancient Rome, in the underground chambers of the Coliseum. The gigantic structure was built in the matter of two years by Augustus Cesar, to entertain the Roman Lords. This structure is not only complete with its underground water drainage system, underground food storage cum provisioning and multifarious storage systems for the underground living quarters, accommodating thousands of gladiators, for their living, equipment storage, feeding, bathing and their rest areas. This structure also enclosed similar areas for the animals that were caged in the Coliseum.

We were shown the underground place for the wild animals and the ventilation system. The Coliseum is still, till this date, is an engineering marvel. It is spread over more than 3000sqm, spanning an area of 7000 buildings, carefully reconstructed with its full detail. We were taken from the dampness of Emperor Commodus' tunnel to the perfectly reconstructed walls decorated with stunning frescoes, from the darkness that swallowed up the breath of the gladiators to the symbols that made that civilization eternal. Leading edge technology, historic research coupled with scientific rigors, made possible this once-in-a-lifetime view of ancient Rome, memorably reconstructed and brought to life in this 3D experience. It was entertaining and yet funny.

We participated in the spectacular gladiatorial games at the fabricated Coliseum. After a stroll along the busy Roman Forum, we walked along the ancient sites of the famous chariot race as depicted in the Hollywood movie "Ben Hur". Finally, we were taken to our overnight hotel, Selene, for a well deserved night's rest.

Sharp at 8 AM, after breakfast, our tour commenced for the day. We were proceeding to the awe-inspiring Vatican. Today on an Easter Sunday, it is a memorable day for Roman Catholics. On this special occasion, the ordained Pope Benedict XVI makes his august appearance before the common people of Rome. His Holiness is the supreme authority of the Roman Catholic order. He was majestically seated on his ceremonial throne at the Vatican square delivering the Easter sermon to his followers, who comprise of the largest Christian community of the world. His pious thoughts were being patiently heard by a million Catholics present at the square with olive branches in hand and piety in their thoughts. We were told that many a millions would be at various Roman Catholic churches or can stay at their home, close to the TV or sit at a public viewing point, straining to hear the sermon at the square on the resurrection of Christ the Lord who was their savior. The Christians always believe that Jesus Christ is the true Son of God, ordained to heal the sufferings and to guide the people and grant strength to them to bear up all sufferings. What a memorable day this is for the believer of Jesus Christ.

# VETICAN

## The Vatican State

We finally drove past the Castle Santa Angelo to the Vatican, the world's smallest nation. We have heard so much about the citadel of Roman Catholic faith and about the construction of St. Peter's Basilica which is the world's largest cathedral. What amazed us were its imposing size, beauty and splendor. The building itself is truly impressive; it is 218 meter long. The Basilica's dome, designed by Michelangelo, is said to be the largest dome in the world measuring 42m in diameter and reaching 138 meter high (more than 450ft). Some of the most celebrated works in the church are the Pieta by Michelangelo, the Papal Altar and the Throne of St. Peter, both by Bernini another famous artist of the Renaissance period. The present State of Vatican is the sole surviving remnant of the Papal States. At one point of time, it occupied thousands of square kilometers in Italy. During the 19th century movement for Italian unification, most of the area of the Papal States was absorbed into Italy. The Lateran Treaty of 1929 set up an independent state of Vatican.

St. Peter's Basilica

## Guided City Tour of Rome

Rome is one of the ancient cities of the world. The roads are fairly broad and well maintained. Not many policemen are seen around, but social offenders are heavily fined. People generally wear ordinary clothes. It is not particularly easy to identify the rich from the poor. A large number of needy people from the third world countries have found their way to this lucrative city. We were warned about the many pickpockets and antisocial elements one had to take personal care of our belongings such as cash, passport, jewelery and valuable documents and told that there were many instances of conman cheating innocent tourists. Therefore it was better that we always move in groups and in known territory. People of Italy or for that matter the entire European mainland generally do not speak English, so it is always better to move with somebody who knows the local language. The local people are exceedingly obliging, helpful and respectful. Roads are spotlessly clean. There are ample snack and beer restaurants spread across the open pavements along the roads and lanes where people generally relax after the hard day's work sipping beer, gossip or simply watch others. Charges are generally double of that what is inside the restaurant.

We moved briskly astride our local guide, almost glued and to the gentleman as he narrated the history of ancient Rome. He was meticulously correlating places with events of the past. He was a small framed Italian dressed in the ancient Roman attire, looked splendidly Roman, energetic, and full of witty remarks and had a convincing grasp over the history of Roman Empire. I later learnt that he was a professor of history in a university at Rome. He would glare into our eyes while amusing us with merry anecdotes of the Roman lords and the indecency of their beautiful ladies at their baths and frequent banquets. Our guide gradually eased his space and reverently strolled as we proceeded to see Piazza Venetia and the colossal Victor Emmanuel II Monument which was built to commemorate the 50th anniversary of Italian reunification. Mr. Marcos, our guide, relived the thrills of historic Rome as we viewed the ancient Roman & Imperial Forums. Thereafter we came face to face with the gigantic Coliseum – the symbol of Rome. It is said that when the Coliseum falls, Rome will fall, and the world will follow.

A view of Colosseum

## Trivia Fountain

We were taken to the famous Trivia fountain, where we were facing the fabulous white marble sculptures of Roman Gods and Goddesses and some of the other deities that donned the front face of an alluring building which was adding to the majestic background to the place. At its front, on a raised platform, in the centre of an open space stood a magnificent awe inspiring sculpture of a majestically poised warrior incarnate above the site of the fountain of water oozed out from below. On both sides and to its rear were a few smaller sculptures with prominent sculptures of two daunting horses on either side, at the feet of the central figure. Those beautiful horses were gasping and struggling to be freed from the iron grip on the reins by the burly horsemen, denoting the hold over the people by the Roman Lords. Around this awe inspiring tabloid was a pool of water from the sacred fountain. This place one of the main tourist attractions in Rome. The perennial fountain has a Roman legend, assuring your return to Rome, if you throw a coin over your left shoulder into the fountain pool. We prayed and threw a coin each and visited a church nearby. We are still waiting for the day of fulfillment of that wish.

The excursion was refreshing and as well revealed to us the bygone days of the city of Rome, and about the ancient Roman Empire. My father had visited Italy during the 2nd World War with the Allied Forces. Till this day, he carried sweet memories of the charming people of the land. My poor impression of them was on account of my professional studies of the military campaigns in the region. But, I think it's never too late to make amend and get to know more about the people and the land. We finally bade farewell to Rome and drove along the picturesque western coast of Italy. Our coach moved into the mysterious Tuscany plateau of the erstwhile Roman Empire. We reached a beautiful town somewhere between Pisa and Florence, for a late night dinner and a well deserved rest in the comforts of our suit at hotel Moderno.

At the Trivia Fountain

# Pisa

## By Road to Pisa

We were out of bed long before the morning wake-up call. The two of us walked out to enjoy the early morning fresh air of the Tuscany hills to be rewarded with many panoramic landscapes views, vibrant display of colorful flowers and decorative plants. The scene was indeed breathtaking. We returned to the hotel to find many of our tour members already assembled. We exchanged few words while moving to the spacious buffet hall for an early morning breakfast. The place was bustling with tourists at the numerous serving counters displaying a variety of continental delicacies. The aroma and sight of delicious preparations stirred up my appetite. Our Jain friends too were not disappointed to find pure vegetarian spread laid out for them. With a bowl of porridge and a platter filled with gourmet of our liking, we sat with a group of friends and enjoyed our food. Breakfast done, we pocketed an apple each for later consumption. The air outside was not too crisp but pleasantly soothing.

I was getting used to the idea of checking out before 8 AM. Mario was there to greet us at his coach. While the bus was moving to Pisa, Amit was narrating the schedule of the day. Eventually a group of spirited young honeymoon couples in our group took the initiative to break the ice by moving to the head of the bus and contacted Amit our Tour Manager, took the mike from him and announced, "Can we have some fun!!" Spontaneous roars of "YES" from all on board led to a carefree rollicking session of icebreaking games. Moods changed, and all joined in for a hilarious session of self introductions, jokes, and merrily sharing some of their personal anecdotes. Everybody was in a happy mood.

The vehicle smoothly rolled down the picturesque Tuscany plateau, winding its way to yet another feature offering fresh vista of the countryside laden with orchards and vine yards. We finally reached our destination at the "Field of Miracles" wherein stands the 12th century Pisa styled marble Cathedral, the Baptistery and the leaning bell tower; which is known throughout the world as the Leaning Tower of Pisa. The vehicle gradually came to a halt. Some of us, on account of the long journey had cramps on our legs and were lamenting our miseries. We gradually streamed out of the bus to be accosted by groups of Bangladeshi hawkers displaying their wide range of ornamental goods, dangling from their hands, neck, shoulder and strands of multi colored beads were draped around their waste. Some of them had many fascinating items in their small bags which were also dangling from their shoulders. The ladies in particular irresistibly stared at those enticing items. It was a comical sight for many of us. This sort of trend is a common practice by hawkers at many places of tourism in India. As we were moving around to get a glimpse of the miracle vistas, Amit assembled us and cautioned us not to get too intimate with the hawkers as they were sharp and cunning pickpocket. Many of us were generally aware of the historical importance of Pisa; nevertheless Amit's efforts were appreciated.

## History of Pisa

Amit's narration of the history of Pisa commencing sometime in180 BC on the banks of Arno River, approximately 10 miles inland from the Liguria Sea, known as a Roman colony. For many years the people there enjoyed a peaceful life. Christianity was embedded into their daily living pattern and into their hearts. A period of aggressions commenced through 800 AD. Because of their prosperity the peace loving Pisa's were repeatedly raided by various enemies including Vikings, Barbarians, Byzantines and Larcenies right up to the 12th century. Ultimately the Pisa's were able to maintain control of their territory and develop lucrative trading activities with Spain and North Africa. In the 12th century, the Pisa supported the Vatican in the 1st Crusade. History of the land between 1228 and 1254 was the accounts of the ongoing skirmishes between Pisa and Florence. The Pisa's were able to maintain upper hand until the armies of Florence finally overcame Pisa. In 1284, the battle of Melaria proved to be the most devastating loss in the history of Pisa. A large number of ships were lost along with more than 11000 men that were killed in the battle.

## Field of Miracles

The field of miracles began to take shape in 1118. In this year, the Cathedral (Duomo in Italian) was consecrated by Pope Gelasius II. In 1153 work began on the Pisa Baptistery. In 1172, after another 20 years, a widow of a wealthy Pisano merchant donated '60 coins' to the church for building the marvelous Bell Tower. Though not completed, the first commission to investigate the tilt of the Leaning Tower (Bell Tower) was formed in 1298. At that time, the tower was leaning at an angle of 1.5 degrees. As time passed, the tower continued to tilt further. In 1370, the tilt was 1.7 degrees. The tilt continued. It is fascinating to note that Galileo Galilee, born in 1564 had moved to Pisa to begin teaching mathematics at the University of Pisa. Galileo conducted his legendary experiment on gravitational forces by dropping objects from the Leaning Tower. Finally, he became a supporter of Copernican theory of the solar system, for which he was persecuted by the Church.

During the19th and 20th century, the Leaning Tower of Pisa proved to be a powerful attraction fueling the city's tourism based economy. It was finally confirmed that the shifting subsoil on which the tower stood had caused the tilt, as the structure could not uniformly withstand the pressure of the construction above it. The tower's foundation has been reengineered, and it is currently thought to be stabilized at that angle. In 1999, soil extraction was performed. That proved to be the definitive solution to the tower. In 1902, the bell tower in Venice's St. Mark's Square collapsed generating fresh concern over the notable instability of the Leaning Tower of Pisa. A worldwide survey was conducted of churches, towers and buildings which were leaning at an angle so as to disprove the miracle aspect. It was discovered that there were many leaning churches on the Rhine river belt of Germany. Some of them were far more precariously tilted than the Leaning Tower of Pisa and yet continue to be places of worship of the fellow Christians.

## Orientation Tour of Pisa

No sooner Amit had finished his recorded talks on Pisa, and then the assembly dispersed. We gradually moved in small groups and at times as couples. We trudged along a bumpy path bustling with tourists all moving towards a common direction. Either side of this winding pathway was occupied by shanty shopkeepers displaying attractive items. Quite a large crowd was thronging the shops. This place was like any place of tourism in India. We could hear shopkeepers cajoling, heckling and perhaps coaxing the customers to buy their products. Some time there were rifts between shopkeepers of different communities, which had to be sorted out by the security people. These shop owners were the economically needy lot from different parts of the world including Europe. These shanty shop owners operated in their mutually agreed domains of operation. They live in their own communes and help each other in the time of grave needs. From time immemorial this appears to have been the practice adopted by shopkeepers, tradesmen and labor-forces immigrating to an economically prosperous land.

We continued to walk and finally faced a high wall built perhaps before the middle ages. As we walked past the arched entrance to the wall, we faced the picturesque "Field of Miracles", which eventually were, the beautiful 12th century white marble structures gleaming in the sun light. There were three distinct structures, a baptistery, a cathedral and a leaning tower. Nearest to us was the Pisa Baptistery which was monumental, beautiful and full of marvelous carvings, it had two distinct patterns of architectures as it was built and then remodeled by different architects for almost three centuries. The result was a grandiose hotchpotch we enjoy seeing even to this day.

The next structure that dominated in the area was the glorious Pisa Cathedral. It was yet another splendid piece of architecture. I continued gazing upon this magnificent Pisa structure made of sparkling white Italian marble. The arches had ornamental designs and exquisite figures carved on it. I could see devotees trickling out of the chapel with Bible in their hands clasped close to their bosom. This picture kept me spellbound for a while and finally I looked up and beyond the magnificent structure. I saw a clear blue sky with a few flakes of silvery clouds at far-off distances. Gradually the clouds were converging above the stupendous building that was the cathedral. The sun's rays pierced through the gaps in the silvery clouds which were gathering above and showered a splendid golden aura on to the Cathedral. To me this was, as though a miracle, showering blessings from heaven above. The spectacle before me was just stunning. I do not remember as to when I looked around to face other friends, to the most of the spectators the sight of the golden glow on the Cathedral was certainly a striking picture to look at and may be an excellent photographic composition, but no more. We moved inside the majestic Pisa Cathedral. It contains a large collection of Roman coffins of stone and some walls still had some ancient frescos left, the most striking one was the triumph of death. The cathedral in Pisa is perhaps the prettiest in Tuscany. Its interior work was made of green and cream marble, with some superb stained glass windows, perched high on the walls. Diffused sun's rays stream through these windows, imbuing the interior with a heavenly aura. The interior of the main hall has many columns, pillars and bronze doors. If St. Peter's in Rome had Michelangelo, Pisa Cathedral had Giovanni Pisano and his masterworks on the pulpit. The most surprising thing in the cathedral was the mosaic of Christ in Majesty, high above the altar. Visitors can see it clearly from a distance.

At this moment as I am putting my thoughts to words I am impelled to describe the inside of this Cathedral in a nutshell which is a Christian place of worship. Like any other cathedral the Pisano-gothic structure from within was a large hall, its large dome is supported by stupendous pillars and archways. At the east end is an arched window with richly tinted glass panels, just below it is the magnificent high altar with the vestry at one flank, which is a room in the church, used as an office and for changing into ceremonial dress, the choir stalls at the other flank. In the middle, of the hall is the sprawling congregation area, that is, the place where one kneels, facing the altar, to offer prayers? From the centre of the hall, one could look-around to see the grandeur and splendor of the murals on the walls and on the ceilings depicting the Christian beliefs.

The spectacle before me as I moved out was equally pleasing. In between the baptistery and the cathedral was the cemetery, which means holy-field. It was so called because the building is believed to be constructed with sacred soil from Jerusalem that was brought in by the archbishop of Pisa in the 12$^{th}$ century.

## Leaning Tower of Pisa

The last and the most unusual structure in the square was, naturally leaning at an angle yet majestically rising up to the clear blue sky above was the Leaning Tower of Pisa. It was supposed to be the bell tower of the cathedral. Having feasted upon this Wonder of the World from where Galileo made his splendid discoveries. I had the urge to climb it but was unable to do so because it needed advance booking!

Beyond the lawn that is the holy-field, were two extraordinarily distinctive museums – Museum Delle Senopie, which had an unusual collection of brown sketches in the wall, used as outlines for the glorious frescos in the rest of the buildings. These 'Sinopie' are the best ways to learn how frescoes are created. The other, Museo Dell Opera Del Duomo, had an unusual collection of artwork from the Cathedral, the Leaning Tower and the Baptistery. Our eyes feasted upon the Fields of Miracle', we finally moved around the stalls appreciating the exquisite mementoes. We had spent quite a few hours there and it was time for us to move on to Florence.

Pisa Cathedral Leaning Tower of Pisa

# Florence

## History of Florence

The vehicle moved on. We were now travelling from Pisa eastward along river Arno to Florence in North-Central Italy. The coach moved on and on. During Julius Caesar's reign in the year 59 B.C. Romans established Florence as a colony along the narrowest stretch of the Arno River at the point where the famous "Ponte vecchio", which is a stone bridge, crosses the Arno River. After conquering, the Romans established Florence, as a key trading centre around the 3rd century A.D. In the 5th century, the peaceful and prosperous lives of these early Florentines came to an abrupt end as the Roman Empire of the West crumbled before the waves of Barbarian conquerors coming from northern Europe. The Dark Ages had begun, and with it was lost Italian unity for nearly 1400 years.

During these hard times, Italian forces in the 8th century crushed the last of the Barbarian kings of Italy. But, this period was short lived. In giving thanks to the local ruler, Pope Leo III made a terrible mistake that led to another prolonged period of disharmony and conflict. To secure the ruler's loyalty, the Pope gave him the title of Holy Roman Emperor. Most of Italy came under the rule of the Emperor, and this led to future conflicts between the Emperor and the Pope that was to drive the Italians into their own version of a civil war. The population of Florence was divided over their loyalty between the two factions. And so in Florence different factions emerged, some Guelf who supported the Emperor, and some Ghibelline who followed the Pope.

In the following centuries, control of Florence changed hands between the Guelfs and Ghibellinesse. As blood flowed on the city streets, families built towers for protection from their enemies within the city. At the end of the 13th Century, the Guelfs were in control, their internal conflicts led to their demise. Typical of the innovative skills and determination of the Tuscan's, throughout this turbulent history the region and Florence enjoyed a booming economy with a population of over 100,000 people. The mainstay of the local economy thrived in wood trade.

## Renaissance Period

At the end of the 14th Century, led by members of the wealthy merchant class, political life in Florence became the realm of artists and intellectuals that planted the seeds for the birth of the Renaissance. During this period, the Medici family rose to power, as leaders of Florence. Their dynasty lasted nearly 300 years. Cosimo de' Medici was a successful banker who endowed religious institutions with artworks. During the reign of his grandson Lorenzoll Magnifico, Florence was caught by an artistic and intellectual fervor that created the Renaissance movement. After the Renaissance, in the following centuries Florence was ruled by a series of ineffective leaders.

During the reunification of Italy in the 19th century it was made temporarily capital of Italy, until Rome finally joined the newly created Italy. Like us, people visit Florence to see the works of Michelangelo, Leonardo da Vinci, Dante, Botticelli, Donatello and many others who helped to change the world of art forever. Thankfully, the last of the Medici, Anna Maria who died in 1743, arguably gave the greatest gift to the city of Florence - in her will she bequeathed all the Medici property to the city on the agreement that they would never leave the city. We moved on; finally the bus stopped at an open space beneath a large four-storied building. There were few other shops and eating places around the parking area. Amit guided us to an Indian Restaurant for a hurried lunch to be in time for our visit to Florence, the birth place of the Renaissance.

## Our Guide for the Tour of Florence

On reaching the city centre, we saw many prominent structures of the middle-ages and were marveling the structures and inquiring about the significance of those buildings. Amit appeared from nowhere with our local guide of the day. She was a charming middle aged comely dressed "mamma mio". By appearance she was a pagan beauty like Venus the Roman Goddess of love. She had her left hand stretched above her shoulder clasping a dainty umbrella as she moved gracefully, her luscious hazel hair bounced in unison with the rhythmical movement of her body as though flaunting her grizzly haired observers. Two strips of red and yellow ribbons dangled from the top of her conspicuous umbrella which occasionally flirted in the breeze, perhaps once again seeking the attention of the observers. She could speak fluent English with a typically Italian accent adding grace to her affable nature. My admiration for her rose fourfold because of her spontaneous response to queries and her profound knowledge of the history of the Renaissance. She glided past the edifice of historic time; spoke fast, passionately about those people, places and their significance in the history of Italy. She was being followed as the rats did the pied-piper. I switched on the voice recorder and carefully listened, observed and photographed the places or the objects she was narrating rather than taking copious notes. Many of the men were astounded at her as she honestly clarified their queries and returned their gaze with a mischievous smile. I observed her again and thought, perhaps she was a replica of Minerva the Goddess of Wisdom, crafts and perhaps war. My mind was floating back and forth from Helen of Troy to the events leading to the Battle of Troy and its final outcome.

## Basilica of St Mary of the Flower

We humbly followed our pied-piper as she guided us to the impressive Duomo which was often referred by the locals as the Cathedral Santa Maria or in English Basilica of St Mary of the Flower. Its original Church was made of wood and dates back to the 7$^{th}$ century. The present structure commenced construction in 1296 and was completed in 1436. It is a marvelous gothic style structure, with perhaps the largest Basilica dome in the world.

I was agog watching all of those magnificent structures from the open space between the buildings. Having entered the Duomo…. I was thankful to the renaissance artists and the people of Florence for preserving every piece of the work of art that lay within those awe inspiring structures. The captivating murals were conveying messages each on different aspects of spirituality. Hanging from the walls were the paintings by distinguished artists of the renaissance period. Exquisitely structured domes and the world reckoned sculptures preserved till this day, for our enjoyment. Each one of the work of art had a story to tell of that period and ages before. I shall later endeavor to bring before the reader some of the significant historic events shaping the destiny of Florence. I have also taken extensive photographs of Florence in order to keep my memory refreshed.

## Baptistery of Florence

We next visited the nearby octagonal shaped Baptistery of Florence. This Baptistery is dedicated to Saint John the Baptist and is one of the oldest buildings in Florence. In the middle Ages, it was believed to be a Roman pagan temple dedicated to Mars. Its balanced geometrical layout and decorations in white and green marble architecture were developed between the 11$^{th}$ to 13$^{th}$ centuries. The external sculptures and works above the doors and on the doors themselves are the most significant works ever made in Tuscany. The gilded bronze doors were made respectively by Andrea Pisano in 1336 the door facing south, north and east by Lorenzo Ghiberti from 1427 to 1452. The latter door is known with the name of Gate of "Paradise" and represents one of the best artistic results ever achieved by the artist. There are many marble sculptures above the doors "Preaching of the Baptist", "Beheading of the Baptist" and the "Baptism of Christ", which were by a great artist. In addition to the inlaid floor the interior displays, some large mosaics on the large dome and the ceiling. All the mosaics have a gilded background and were made between middle of 13th century and the beginning of the 14th century.

Baptistery of Florence

# Palazzo Vecchio and Loggia del Lanzi

The 14th century Palazzo Vecchio with its imposing Tower was our next stop. At this point, our guide looked more like Goddess Venus than Diana. This fortress was the seat of the civil power of Florence. Its lower courtyard with adjoining chambers was the town hall of Florence. This massive, Romanesque fortress palace with its majestic tower is among the most impressive town hall of Tuscany. Its entrance overlooks the Piazza with Michelangelo's statue of David, flanked by Baccio Bandinella's Hercules and

Cacus. Those two sculptors face the gallery of statues in the adjacent Loggia del Lanzi. Palazzo Vacchio is a magnificent building from inside with its first, second and third courtyards richly adorned with artistic accomplices of ages past on the roofs, walls, pillars and in every part of its spacious rooms.

We moved out of the Palazzo Vacchio and faced the magnificent sight of Loggia Lanzi Palazzo. It is one of the most significant public places in Italy, an open air museum sufficient to one city to be called a town of art. It was originally built between 1376 – 1382 to house the assemblies of people and hold public ceremonies like swearing in of officials. The vivacious construction of Loggia is in stark contrast with the severe architecture of the Palazzo Vacchio. It is effectively an open-air sculpture gallery of antique and Renaissance art. Amongst many Roman sculptures is the Rape of the Sabina Woman, Pursues with the head of Medusa, Medica Lions and other Renaissance and later arts kept at this place. We moved on to Ponte Vacchio and then to the Museum of Galileo.

Sculptures at Loggia del Lazia like Ersis with head of Medusa and others

## Ponte Vacchio

Ponte Vecchio is Florence's most distinctive bridge on the Arno River. It is a medieval bridge over the Arno River. The bridge still remains to this day. The houses and shops built along it as was once common in the early days. Florence on the banks of Arno River was a thriving business centre in the 11th century. Butchers initially occupied the shops. The present tenants are jewelers, art dealers and souvenir sellers. It has been described as Europe's oldest wholly-stone closed segmental arched bridge. Rather than its looks it is of historic importance.

## Museum Galileo

This museum holds Galileo's work. His discoveries and instruments are on display. It is also intriguing to see how he thought out how to demonstrate motion, balance, force etc. We all bade farewell to our guide, a true replica of the Goddess of wisdom and we walked on the pavements along river Arno. As we moved upstream to reach our bus and Mario a mile or so away, I noticed a number of museums, art shops and eating places across the road on the left of us, but did not have the energy or a strong inclination to walk into any one of them. Finally, one more grueling day of sightseeing and delving into the history of Italy was over. We drove towards Venice, the romantic Italian city. Our overnight stay was at hotel Park Villaflorita in Padova, Italy.

# Venice

## How Venice Was Born

In the olden days Venice was known as Serenissima Republican. It was a powerful state. Marco Polo was from Venice, and he was the first European merchant to open the Silk Road to China. St. Mark's was from here. The cultural journey of Venezia never ends so let me explain some of the historic facts from its foundations to the present day Venice.

According to tradition, Venice was founded in 421 AD. The most central village in the lagoon in those days was not Venice but Torcello. In 639, a Cathedral was built where many people seeking refuge from the barbarian invasions had been taking shelter. Time elapsed, and step by step Venice emerged out of the several islands of the lagoon, linked by bridges. In Venice, the Doges' government was established in 726. The year 814 was the starting date of the construction of Palazzo Ducale (Doges' Palace) in what is today St. Mark's Square. The Basilica St. Mark's was begun in 834, but this first basilica was burnt down. Venice was spreading its commercial boundaries, and in 1000, its fleet defeated the pirates of the Adriatic Sea. Venice took part in the Crusades war campaigns, aimed to free Jerusalem.

Many works of art were taken to Venice as booty, for instance the four bronze horses of St. Mark's. The original bronzes can now be seen in St. Mark's museum, whilst the four horses on the Basilica's facade are perfect copies. The journey of the Venetian merchant Marco Polo from Venice to China in the 13th century is one of the most fascinating true stories of the middle ages. His adventures and meeting with Chengis Khan are well remembered. In 1348, Venice population was halved by the plague, in spite of this Venice succeeded in becoming the leader of the 4 sea powers of Mediterranean Sea: the other ones were the Republics of Amalfi, Genoa and La Spezia In 1489 Venice conquered the island of Cyprus. Another notable plague affected Italy. Another fact is that Giacomo Casanova, is not a legend: he was born in 1725 in Venice, the myth of the irresistible seducer and lover as narrated in his own words in the book Memories di Giacomo Casanova', are true accounts of his misadventures. Venice was defeated by Napoleon in 1797, and it became a part of the Hapsburg Empire (Austria).

## Venice the City of Canals

After having dwelled on the history of Venice, I shall now narrate our activities of the day commencing after a continental breakfast and the routine checking-out of hotel Park Villaflorita which was on the mainland just across Venice. Mario drove us to the boat waiting at the ferry. As we passed he pointed at the Mussolini's Bridge of Liberty and said Mussolini was a curse to his community and to the people of Italy. I seem to agree with him on this score at least. A ferryboat carried us across the lagoon to the main island of Venice. Over the years, Venice has now expanded to an archipelago of 118 islands, 170 canals and about 400 bridges.

We were busy viewing the panoramic scenes all around us. The boat picked up speed and maneuvered past many elegant cruise liners and many other gorgeously luxury boats anchored along the embankments on either side of our speeding river-craft. Our boat went past many grandiose buildings of the middle-age which were touching the water line. Some of us took photos sauntering from one end of the deck to the other end for better camera views. This absurd behavior surely must have amused many of the passengers sitting and were the regular passengers on the ferry to

Venice. Few of us climbed to the top deck to get wider panoramic view of the lagoon. The views were a life time experience for many like the two of us. After about half hour of boat ride along the scenic main lagoon, we reached the central island of Venice. The boat moored at a ferry point. Amit ploughed his way past the touring crowd to a prominent spot on a cemented platform and beckoned our group to follow him.

A boat ride along the main lagoon of Venice

## Bridge of Sighs

Our first stop was at the Bridge of Sighs, which was a small arched bridge over a narrow canal joining two lofty medieval buildings on either side. The bridge was concrete cement structure covered from the top and sides. It had two small windows facing us. This notorious place was named Bridge of Sighs, as it was from these windows a prisoner had his last look of Venice and smelled its fresh air. Once inside the underground murky prison cell the unfortunate prisoner would be doomed for life and never to meet a visitor or see the light of day ever after. A jail warden had narrated that the prisoners were huddled in groups or singly in small, stinking, dark, damp, unhygienic, foul smelling underground cells with small ventilators high up near the ceiling. Daring the harshness of this place and in-spite of the tight security measures at all hours, the adventurous Giacoma Casanova, who was once dishonored and imprisoned there, escaped from his prison cell. This daredevil feat could only be made possible by him alone because of his grit, determination and cunningness. He had managed to escape from his dungeon through the heavily guarded ventilators, and jumped down from the steep wall to see the light of day. He was finally pardoned and lived to continue his romantic escapades.

## St. Mark's Square

St. Mark's Square (Piazza San Marco) is at the very heart of Venice. This square was called, 'the drawing room of the world' by Napoleon. This place has been the centre of religions and social life in the Venice republic for over thousands of years. At this place one sees the splendor of the St. Mark's Basilica, the artistic beauty and the historic Ducal Palace with its infamous old Prison cells under it and many more structures of which I shall mention now. As we moved on along the famous St. Mark's Square, we saw the exquisite Clock Tower (Bell tower), and many other prominent landmarks which I shall mention later. It is necessary to note that the original Clock Tower was leaning like the Leaning Tower of Pisa and in 1902; it came crumbling down to a heap of stones, also raising doubts about the future of the Leaning Tower of Pisa.

The magnificent St. Mark's Basilica is perhaps the most well known building in the heart of Venice. The original church was built between the years 829 to 836, as a timber construction and in 976, it was burnt down. It was again rebuilt between the years 1043 to 1070, at the same location of the burnt church. The present Basilica was built like a Byzantine structure ultimately having 5 domes and the construction was completed in 1094. However, it took many centuries to complete the marvelous decoration of its facade and interiors. Many aspects of St Mark's Basilica are closely related to parts of the Piazza (St. Mark's Square) including the whole of the west facade with its illustrious arches and marble decoration, the Roman carvings round the central doorway and above all, the four horses which preside over the whole piazza and such potent symbols of pride and power of Venice that its ruler in 1379 said that there could be no peace between the two cities until these horses had been bridled. Four hundred years later, Napoleon, after he had conquered Venice, had them taken down and shipped two horses to Paris. While moving on the St. Mark's Square (Piazza) as we walked away from the Basilica, we started by crossing the open space on the north side of the church named after the two marble lions presented by Doge monarch in 1722, on which children are often scrambling.

St. Mark's Basilica and other prominent
structures around St. Mark's Square

Beyond the church, we came across the famous Clock Tower of Venice, completed in 1499, above a high archway where the street known as the main thoroughfare of the city leads through shopping streets to the Rialto, which is the commercial and financial centre of Venice. To the right of the clock tower is a closed church, sometimes open for exhibitions. Turning left and following the long arcade along the north side of the Piazza. In the days of the Republic of Venice, the buildings we were now facing was formerly known to be the homes and offices of the Procurators of Saint Mark and other high officers of the state. They were built in the early 16th century.

The arcade is lined with shops and restaurants at ground levels now, with offices above. The restaurants include the famous Café Quadri where the two of us rested for a while but dared not to order for coffee. This is the exact place patronized by the Austrians when Venice was ruled by Austria in the 19th century, while the Venetians preferred Florians, a restaurant on the other side of the Piazza. Turning left as we had reached the end, the arcade continues along the west end of the Piazza, which was rebuilt by Napoleon in 1810 and is known as the Napoleonic Wing. It holds behind the shops a ceremonial staircase leading to a royal palace, but now forms the entrance to the Correr Museum. Turning left again, the arcade continues down the south side of the Piazza. The buildings on this side were designed in the mid 16th century but partly built in 1582-6 and finally completed by1640. The ground floor has shops and also the famous Café Florian.

We visited the Murano Glass Factory; a master craftsman demonstrated the art of creating the famous Venetian blown glass. Some of our friends did not miss this opportunity to buy souvenirs at specially discounted prices. I was obsessed with the wan in which the craftsman was blowing into a long pipe dipped into the molten silicon and dexterously shaping crystal glass articles of use and for home decoration. Later we moved as couples or small group's site seeing the places of our interest, moving from island to island connected by the bridges. Whereas many were taking rides on the gondolas. We were freely walking and observing others enjoying. We had an urge for a romantic ride on a gondola with a handsome oarsman with his mandolin softly humming a romantic Italian tune. As he sang with a deep throated masculine voice, the mandolin tingling as the background music, building up the crescendo to a romantic urge to sail across the silvery moon. Unfortunately, we were not carrying the expenses for the ride. There were many other attractions around the place including expensive jeweler items. My wife got interested and was about to negotiate a price, but after second thought declined the purchase. Time then was almost 12 noon and we were to return to the ferry soon. Amit was urging every one of us to reach the ferry point or else we would miss the waiting ferryboat. The next ferryboat is to leave after 2 hours, and our bus is scheduled to leave from shore for our next destination within 40 minutes time then. All of us happily boarded the ferry and finally moved to our coach, and began speeding towards Innsbruck, Austria.

# AUSTRIA

## Journey to Innsbruck

Time was past 12.45 PM, and we were on our last leg of the journey from Italy to Austria, but we had not yet enjoyed a pure Italian meal. Amit advised us against eating local food stuff to be physically fit for the remaining 12 days of our hectic travel in Europe. However, he told us that delicious Italian meals were available at the nearby restaurants and, we were free to experiment at our personal expenses. We hurriedly gulped our meals to be back in the coach by 1.30 PM. so as to travel the remaining 250 km over the rugged Alpine ranges to reach Innsbruck by 5 PM. Most of us had enjoyed a fabulous preparation of pure Punjabi meal in a well furnished Indian restaurant run by a North Indian family. My dream of sitting in an expensive restaurant, in the company of charming gentry enjoying mouthwatering Italian wine and food, at a candlelit table just for two, remained unfulfilled.

After lunch, we continued our journey north over hills, along meadows, crossing valleys and river lines. Miles after miles of the dark, rich soil was laden with acres and acres of grape vines, olive plantations, oranges and many other exotic plants of the Mediterranean region. Our luxury coach moved whereas the majority of us were engrossed in playing silly games and being engrossed in activities like group songs, Ghazals and other heart rendering solo performances by some of our tour members. Not to miss the fun Amit was also heard humming a few of the popular Hindi tunes. Mario did not seem to enjoy the Hindi tunes. His two hands firmly on the wheel he shook his head from side to side with an unusual slur on his usual somber face when a Hindi song was being sung by the group. His vehicle finally lunged into the Austrian Alps and drove downhill to River Inn. As we reached Innsbruck, the majestic Alps could be seen from almost any vantage point in the old town of Innsbruck. As we looked on, climbing to the top of those mountains appeared to be easy on the tarmac road, but somewhat expensive. Several options were available, but the most popular was ascending the mountains right to the north of Innsbruck. A funicular goes from the south bank of the Inn River to the Hungerburg (this area can also be reached by car or on foot). From here, a cable car goes all the way to the top of the Hafelekar peak 7657 ft in the Nordkette Mountains. I realized that Austria was indeed a land of pristine beauty portraying panoramic views of exotic mountain formations.

## Bergisel Ski Jump

Bergisel Ski Jump is of a towering height in the sky above the city and is a strikingly beautiful sight for all to admire. The hill on which this historic Ski Jump site is situated was once the scene of the battles of 1809, in which Tyrolean peasants fought against French in the Tyrolean War of Independence. The first ski jump was built here in the 1925 and later its construction was improved in stages to a spectacular new ski jump as it exists today, which is regarded as a tourist attraction that should not be missed by visitors to Innsbruck. The Tower stands forty-seven meters tall and provides spectacular views. The new facilities can now house about thirty thousand spectators. The Innsbruck Ski Jump is a common venue for the Winter Olympic Ski Jumping.

After an interesting drive over the Austrian Alps, we reached Innsbruck. At 5 in the evening, the sun was well above the western sky. Amit lead us on an orientation tour of the Old City where lies the Goldenes Dachl – the Golden roof, an ornate Gothic balcony, symbol of the city. We saw the 17th Century fountain with the equestrian statue of King Leopold V, St. Anne's Column, the Innsbruck's arch of celebration and grief. We also saw the Heiblinghaus which is a building resembling a wedding cake. Hofburg (Imperial Palace), which served as residence when the Habsburg emperors visited Innsbruck. We then visited the St. Peter's Church and took a long stroll around the New City area, which was well laid out with all modern amenities. We all admired the cleanliness and the meticulous layout of the places. Finally, I got an adrenalin urge to do something remarkable. So, I decided for a sitting with a local roadside artist for making a pencil sketch of me. While the artist was busy with his work of art, a few of the local damsels stooped over the artist's shoulder with an urge to admire his work of art, not realizing the discomfort being caused by them. The artist appeared distracted and was hurrying through his job. My wife, Swapna first persuaded and then she insisted that the artist should complete the sitting early. At the end, the artist made my sketch, in which I looked like an African American scavenger with a goat's beard who was probably sitting in a superficial posture, and nurturing a roguish look. I was annoyed with him and asked him what it was he had made of me. He promptly retorted, Caricature you know! I couldn't control myself and cast a superficial grin but had to pay him my valuable 10 Euros for the obnoxious sketch. He had a laugh, my friends had a bigger laugh at him, and I had quietly turned away. Finally, we checked into a hotel at about 9.30 PM. Dinner was by10.30 and some of us went for a Tyrolean Folklore Show. We wanted to flow with the spirit of Tyrol, and during an evening of traditional entertainment, our moods were sufficiently charged to enjoy every-bit of the authentic folk music accompanying instruments to Tyrolean dancing. We had enjoyed the simultaneous shoe slapping, songs and yodeling, all of which was in traditional Tyrolean dresses. Our overnight stay was at hotel Austrotel in Innsbruck, Austria.

Glimpses of Innsbruck

# Visit to Swarovski Museum

I came out of my room early to find many others from our group already enjoying the early morning glimpses of the snow clad alpine mountains. When I looked I faced a new panoramic picture of the 'Gift of God' to mother-nature. We all finally moved in for breakfast and finally checkout of our hotel. Our first stop for the day was at 20 minutes drive from our hotel to visit the Swarovski Crystal World in Wattens. The artificial hill before us looks like an enormous face, from its mouth spouts a waterfall. The whole Swarovski museum of crystals is built half underground and its roofs are covered with soil and over it a lush green turf, so there is no exterior structure like in other museums. The most surprising exotic beauty was beneath the domineering face shaped hillock, with the set of expressive eyes that could pierce into our minds, the nose was perfectly chiseled and its carefully carved voluptuous mouth was gaping open with white pearly beads of water gushing out to fall into a deep green pool. The entrance and the exits to the museum were on the either side of the huge face, through the doors depicting the earlobes. Inside of the building was a magnificently spacious with its seven linked halls. The entire place was designed in honor of Daniel Swarovski, founder of the biggest producer of crystal in the world. This work of creative-art is by Andrew Heller, and it was opened to public in 1995. Since then it has been a significant attraction for millions of people. The entrance leads to a crystal wall, made of 12 tons of the perfect crystals in the world. Another hall is the "Planet of Crystals" where you will see a magnificent light show. In the Swarovski Crystal world, we saw many artworks by world-known artists - from Andy Warhol to Salvador Dali. There is even a replica of crystal Taj Mahal and a Rajput Maharaja's horse laden with crystal ornamental dressings. We moved into the heart of a crystal in the Crystal Dome and witnessed some spectacular shows in the Crystal Theatre. Each room we had entered had yet a new creation of crystal art.

We finally entered the hall where we could buy some beautiful crystal artworks like small musical instruments, exquisite jewelry and many other works of crystal art. All of us were doing a lot of window shopping. Many among us with business temperaments bought a lot of jewelry to be shipped to their home. A few ladies bought frightfully expensive items. Finally,

I bought Swarovski locket and chain for Swapna's birthday, due on the 12<sup>th</sup> of May. We moved from the crystal world to the alpine garden where we saw some plants typically grown in this part of Austria. There was an extraordinarily entertaining children's playground. Like many other visitors, the younger kids of our group also entered the play ground. Some of them also played hide-and-seek with their parents. Elderly lot were either sitting or lying in groups on the lush green lawns, basking in the sun gossiping and displaying their recent purchases. The commercially inclined men of our group were keenly comparing prices with valued Indian products. The ladies were invariably looking satisfied with their new possessions.

After our rewarding visit to the Swarovski Museum we travelled west-word in the picturesque Austrian Alps; at times along the river lines or over the ridges covered with deep green pine forests and at places the coach almost appeared to be dangling from sharp cliffs or escarpments, then the road meandered along the hills or lunged through the many dozens of mountain tunnels. There were short, long and unusually long tunnels pierced through the tectonic stratum of the gorgeous alpine mountain ranges. The longest tunnel in the region we had crossed was over 14 km long. Each one of those picturesque sights was a dream come true. At places, a view of the snow-capped mountain tops added a fresh fervor to my thoughts.

Some photos of scenic Austria

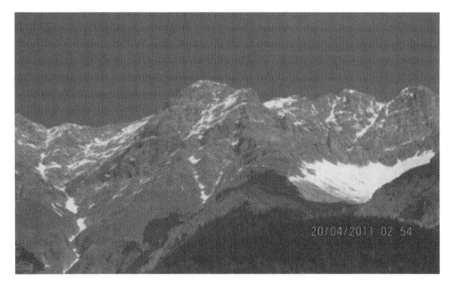

# PRINCIPILITY OF LIECHTENSTEIN

## Vaduz

The coach moved on. None of us spoke. Gradually the geographical layout changed, and we were finally in a richly cultivated valley with the Rhine River flowing parallel on the northern side of the road. At a distance beyond the river, the ground was rising to the hills with acres after acres of grape vines, the hills rose higher to reach the scanty pine trees, thereafter the hills blended further to meet the snow-capped mountain peaks. To our south we could see many acres of cultivated land with cows grazing at places and farmers working in the lush green fields. Thus, we neared Vaduz, the capital of the Principality of Liechtenstein. During the Roman era, it was a part of the Holy Roman Empire. Vaduz is hugely popular with tourist from all over the world for the view of the majestic Castle of Vaduz, its cozy looking hutment, street cafes and vineyards. Actually we had halted there for one more purpose other than sightseeing, and that was to sit together at open spaces for relaxation. We finally sat in small groups, to eat from our packed-lunch, which was provided to us by Amit. Our picnic spot was generally used by tourists and working people who were not from Vaduz to have their meals during their recess. I saw many open air restaurants around this area.

Scenes around Vaduz

Liechtenstein, though it was an exceptionally small principality on a stretch of land, between western part of Austria and the south east portion of Switzerland is a constitutional monarchy with a population of just 37000 permanent dwellers and the rest were the daily waged laborers who daily come from nearby Austria or Switzerland to work in the field, factories and offices. Surprisingly, this tiny state has one of the highest per-capita-income in the world ($157,000). The peculiarity of this small Kingdom is that it is short of manpower. So, every morning, the daily wage workers come from the neighboring countries like Austria, Italy and Switzerland to work in various departments for a specific time in the day. They are permitted to use the recreation areas near to their place of work with many eating places and rest areas to be enjoyed during their off periods, but all of the foreign labor must return to their native land before the sun sets.

The local people of Liechtenstein are also extremely hard-working. They are generally the departmental heads, supervisors and the management heads and control all aspects of finances and administration, apart from running farmhouses, orchards and other technical or administrative functions they are adept at. The people of this tiny community are very good at commerce and export business.They are known to be a world reckoned banking community. Their banking system is considered to be more reliable than the Swiss Banks. Rajiv and Sonia Gandhi have their accounts here. After our lunch, we enjoyed a pleasant walk along the streets and shopping centers of Vaduz. Then we took a Mini train ride around the victorious township and took some pictures the view-points. Finally, we were moving to Zurich. The ride from Vaduz to Zurich over the Swiss Alps was through some of the most beautiful places to see. At times we would see the River Rine deep down in the ravines, peacefully meandering on its course to reach its final destination. Whilst at the next turn we would get a panoramic view of snow-clad Alps, with dark dense pine forest at the lower reaches of the mountains. The entire area was very scantily populated. We perhaps saw a hutment or two alongside some cultivation.

Our journey was not for ling, within two hours we had reached the commercial hub of Switzerland and that is Zurich.

# SWITZERLAND

## Zurich

While we were on the orientation tour at Zurich, we saw the elegant Bahnhofstrasse, the busiest street of Zurich, lined with Banks, shopping arcades and boutiques, then the St. Peter's Church with the largest clock face in Europe and the famous churches of Fraumunster, known for its beautiful stained glass windows created by Marc Chagall and Grossmunster churches with the twin Romanesque towers. We enjoyed walking along the vast lake front, the lake was bustling with steamers; I saw boats returning with passengers and goods were approaching from the further end of the lake, while others remained docked, and waiting their turn to puffing out to sea. At a distance, sailing yachts of varying description, sizes were seen floating across the horizon while others lay at their nearby anchorage. Zurich lake front was indeed a busy place. It was a treat to watch the speedboats whizzing past in front of us with the water skiers holding on to the Cord and cheeringly waived a hand at their admirers. Even at that hour in the evening when the sun was about to be setting on the western horizon, everyone at the waterfront seemed busy enjoying a life of their own without causing any harm or hindrance to others privacy. We, the tourists were also enjoying marveling the panorama, the glistering beauty of the snow-clad Alpine peaks in the distance northwest casting a sunset glow and shadows to remind us of the nearing dusk. We were merrily walking, admiring the astounding architectures of the medieval Europe and talked among ourselves of our earlier visit to the places. Some of us sat to relax while others went shopping and to the worldwide recognized Swiss Banks. Swapna finally decided to sit and chat with ladies.

We moved around the shopping complexes, the magnificent churches and admired the opera houses we had come across during our city tour. Finally, the two of us decided to relax at the waterfront. Swapna moved onto a benches occupied by some of the ladies of our group. I decided to sit alone at the water front to relax and enjoying the activities taking place before me. An elderly person with a cheerful face, perhaps around 60 years sat beside me. He introduced himself as Mr. Mansukani, an Indian citizen on a business trip to Zurich and said that he has been here for the past three months. I understood that he was somewhat involved with the Swiss Stock Exchange. I know terribly little about commercial money-exchange, so our conversation finally turned to other matters of common interest. I was still extremely reticent with this stranger, so I continued conversation in a decidedly cautious manner. Mr. Mansukani, obviously a Sindhi was from Ahmadabad. His wife and two sons were in some sort of business in Mumbai. His younger sibling was yet to marry so he was on the search for a decent bride from any Indian community. Our conversation turned to Zurich. He shared some of his many fascinating experiences, and I learn a terrific deal about the place. I sort of took a liking to him. He was a man of many attributes of which Indian classical music was one of them. We could have continued our discussions for long but as time don't wait so we had to depart. Our tour bus was waiting to move us to our new destination at Engelberg, so we thanked each other for the excellent time spent together. He handed me his business card which I have somehow misplaced. At the appointed time, we boarded our bus to be taken to yet another breathtaking spot 60 km away in the Swiss-alpine mountain ranges.

## Picture from Zurich Lake

The present day Zurich is divided into five districts. In ancient time, the city of Zurich was originally a Roman Customs post. In the past this city had many a master. Geographically Zurich is a piece of land in the south-central Switzerland occupying an area of approximately 92sqkm of which 5 percent of the area is made up of Lake Zurich. River Limmat constitutes the densest populated part of the city. The river is flowing in a south-north direction parallel to it runs River Sihl, which meets with the Limmat at a place near the Swiss National Museum.

Operas, ballets, theaters and many other cultural activities are mainly in the Old City District of Zurich, it has the most of the recognized opera houses. Zurich Opera House is one of the principal opera houses in Europe. Built in 1834, it was the first permanent theatre in Zurich. Those interested in hearing symphony of heart rendering orchestral music, operas and theaters of an exclusively high order should visit one of the many opera houses in the old city district and as well in the West and East districts. Whereas, on this account, the North and South districts are less fortunate compared to the remaining other districts. Night life and clubbing are also in the Old City District. For the grubby slash-dash enthusiasts, Zurich offers an excellent deal of variety when it comes to nighttime leisure. It is the host city of the world famous Street Parade which takes place in August every year. The most famous district for nightlife is at the central parts of the old city. Their social habits are prominently visible in the old city with bars, restaurants, lounges, stylish public habits, clubs, etc. and a lot of fashion shops for the young and stylish public. There are many cheap titillating amusements in Brazilian bars, Caribbean restaurant, pink clubs, Hip Hop stages, Turkish kebabs and Italian espresso coffee bars and also many sex shops or for that matter the famous red-light district of Zurich are in the Old City District.

The bus moved on; finally we reached a sleepy township named Engelburg, nestled in picturesque alpine mountains in central Switzerland. The glimmer of daylight persisted in the western sky. The time at that moment, was well past 9 PM. We hurriedly carted our baggage and took turn in placing our belongings in the luggage lift, to be moved up to the main reception where Amit was handing over the room keys.

By 10.15 PM we were able to settle down in our room with all preparations made for the next day's outing. Within 30 minutes, the two of us entered the dining-hall. Most of us gulped down the soup and hurriedly munched the platter in front of us and brushed out of the buffet hall after a quiet goodnight to those still eating. By the time we reached our room I was rather groggy and was straining to keep my eyes open. Barely did I reach the room I crawled into my bed for a well deserved sleep. Overnight stay was at the beautiful hotel Terrace in Engelberg, Switzerland.

## Engelberg to Lauterbrunnen

I was fresh and agile in the morning. After a continental breakfast, we travelled about 70 km by our bus viewing scenic landscapes around us. The pristine beauty that lay within Switzerland amazed me. The bus we were travelling in was being driven along lakes, ravines, brooks, and occasional near lonely hutment at the edge of a steep hill. The topography was enchanting, and finally we reached Lauterbrunnen. From there, our onward journey was by rail to the snow clad mountain peaks of Jungfraujoch.

# Lauterbrunnen to Jungfraujoch

Our move from Lauterbrunnen to Jungfraujoch was carried out in three stages, each time changing the clog-wheel rails. The trains had comfortable seating arrangements we could converse and enjoy an all round panoramic view through the wide windows. Every time we changed trains, we had to move in the open air and face biting cold breeze, which entered our lungs and sent waves of cold shiver down to every bone in our body. Even daunting those, some of us had stayed out to view the picturesque snow clad mountain features around us. At some of those halts, we viewed the picturesque snow clad mountains from sheltered viewing platforms drilled in the mountain which enabled an all-round vista of the snow clad mountains, sharp cliffs and deep gorges descending to an abysmal depth. Some of those viewing pockets were drenched in the morning sunlight and offered stunning sights. Finally, we boarded our last train to Jungfraujoch. Jungfrau is the mountain peak just below which is the highest railway station in Europe at 11333 ft. To reach there, we had been through an interesting journey along lakes, gurgling streams, escarpments and mountain passes. We all marveled the changing alpine scenery as our Cog-wheel train huffed and puffed to reach us to our unique destination to the top of the Jungfrau peak for our once in a lifetime experience at our age. There have been many like me with similar physical ailments like mine who had daunted the weather to be able to cherish a lifetime dream.

# Jungfraujoch

On reaching Jungfraujoch, we had our lunch at an Indian vegetarian restaurant perched on top of the Jungfrau mountain plateau. While taking meal, we could see just below our restaurant a breathtaking view of Aletsch Glacier. After lunch, we had no respite. With our belly full, we had to move a long distance to view the landscape on the furthermost side of the building. As we moved, I noticed many more eating places, some of them catering for the exclusive eating habits of people from China, Mexico, Thailand, Italy, India and many more countries. Many restaurants served European buffets, buns, pastries, coffee and ice cream. The building complex comprised of three floors, bustling with people of many nationalities of which the Chinese were the maximum. I saw many, tall, rugged looking males and females generally of the European origin. Some of them looked to be either from Georgia or Armenia of the Caucasus mountain region. They were moving unusually fast in their heavy ski-boots with long and heavy ski-blades slung over their shoulders. The skiers were also moving towards the door to the snow-clad plateau in front of the building. We walked along with skiers and reached the open plateau leading to the picturesque twin peaks of Jungfraujoch. There were other features surrounding the Sphinx Terrace. Looking at the breathtaking Jungfrau Peak and the breathtaking Aletsch Glacier from unusually close-up view point constructed for the purpose. Outside the building, we faced biting cold wind. I soon realized that we had to move around or else be a frozen carcass. Irrespective of the harsh weather conditions, panting heavily due to the scarcity of oxygen in the air, I limped but enjoyed this memorable encounter with the eternally snow clad plateau, where the people ski and play with snowballs or rush downhill in sledges. I enjoyed seeing the younger tourists merrily enjoying chasing one another, then falling, and again running, finally to end with a breath taking hug. A spirit of merriment lurked in the air for all present on Sphinx Terrace. We were also moved by the prevailing tempo of activities. As we were moving further away, I was surprised to look back at the imposing restaurant building which I had left far behind me in the distant. It looked magnificent, like a picture from a fairy-tale. It looked as though a beautiful castle has been perched on top of the world by a magnificent builder. We moved and looked around and saw others enjoying. Because of the rarity of oxygen at the height of above 11500ft I was getting breathless, so was my wife. We finally decided not to move any further. We stood and watched for a while and then returned within the comforts of the building. Amit was probably watching from inside and waiting for us. On our return, he guided us down the stairway to the entry point of the Ice Palace.

Photos from Jungfaurjonch

# Ice Palace

Ice Palace is a longish, winding tunnel made of ice. The interior is sufficiently broad to be able to accommodate a group of people moving together within the tunnel. There were a number of protrusions or you may call ice caves which where displaying astounding ice-sculptures. There were many fascinating pockets which arouse interest to those with a liking to sculptures. This tunnel of ice was around a kilometer long but suffocating for those with breathing problems at high altitudes. Our movement was slow, and I was getting suffocated inside the closed tunnel. We walked slowly but, still got breathless, stopped for a while, walked again, took some photographs; thus both of us pressed on, while we saw the younger physically fitter lot was screaming with joy, as they moved across those numerous sculptures made of ice. In about an hour and a half time, we returned safely back to the main building. We both were totally exhausted and plunged on the staircase itself, breathing heavily; finally we shifted to a nearby shelf at the window site. Our chosen seat was comfortable and overlooked the glacier below the windowpane. A few of our friends came inquiring of our health. Finally, I was fit enough to walk and fetch two cups of coffee and biscuits from a nearby counter. The hot coffee had healed me altogether. I walked around the place and took a lot of photographs and was reading some of the write-ups on the walls around the hall. The displays mention that in the year 1893 the Jungfrau Railway lines to the top of the world at Jungfraujoch was initiated by Mr. A Gayer-Zeller. The placards highlights this railroad till this day has been acknowledged by many prominent people as an engineering marvel. An electronic device displayed the present room temperature at -5 degrees Celsius whereas the temperature outside was -10 degrees and at the Ice Palace -8 degrees. No wonder I was literally trembling in the ice terrace. I could send a postcard to my friends from there.

At the Ice Palace

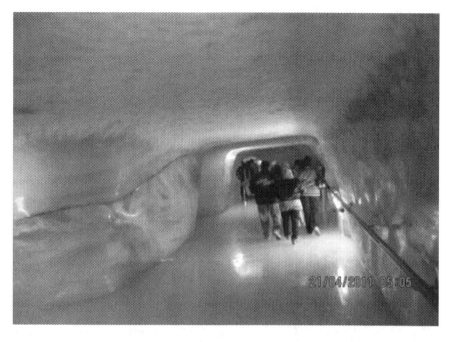

## Interlaken

On our return journey in our dear old cogwheel train, we had an intriguing unspecified halt. As reported to us, the shoe-brakes to the cogwheel of our compartment got jammed. We had to discontinue our sing-song session and get out of the train. There was no specific danger to life, but the dark pine forest in the wilderness where we got down from our train had shrouded the thoughts of many an elder, while others cheerfully played with or collected bags full of dry pinecones which were lying littered all over the ground. We did not have to wait long as our replacement coach arrived within 30 minutes. We finally reached Interlaken, a prominent city of Switzerland's best-known health and pleasure resorts. There was time to relax at the many cafes and shop for Swiss watches, chocolates, etc. The day's excursion was not over as yet. Mario with his beaming smile escorted us to his luxuriant haven to be taken to our abode 50 km away to Engelberg. After an exhaustive day of outing, we returned late in the evening via Interlaken back to our Hotel Terrace. At the hotel, we were entertained with melodious carols and instrumentals by a group of Swiss singers. Many of our group members preferred resting. But we continued to sit till dinner time sipping hot coffee while enjoying the music. Seeing those many opera houses I can now confirm that the Swiss people are exceedingly fond of their music, preferably symphony of pulsating orchestra, operas and as well pop-music.

## Mount Titlis

Early the next morning we did not have to go particularly far to commence our journey to Mount Titlis at 10000 (ft). It is the highest peak in central Switzerland. As we journeyed to Mount Titlis by a series of three different cable car rides, we were amazed to see the scenic change from green meadows, scenic lakes to snow clad mountains. At one stretch, there were over 200 cable cars sporting different flags. I was told to lookout for cable car number 73 that carries the Indian flag! The last leg of the ascent to the world's first rotating cable car called the 'Titlis Rot air' was spacious with glass-paneling for an all round view of the snow-clad mountains.

We reached on top of the breezy snow clad plateau which was just below the peak of the Mt. Titlis. At this particular moment on the plateau at a height of 10000ft, wind was blowing around 60 km per hour; because of the strong wind I was standing firm on both my feet to maintain my body balance. We clung to each other for mutual support. Finally, gained a little more confidence so took courage to move further out onto the plateau where people were standing with the skiing rods for support. We held on to the iron railing precisely laid to guard the skiers from skidding down the hazardous cliffs. To us this place was a heavenly sight. As I stood there motionless, gazing at the mystic haze resembling a blizzard, the sun's rays finally trickling in at places revealing the majestic snow-clad mountain peaks above a layer of clouds which was gradually moving away from us. Very soon the entire place lit up, the breeze subsided, and we had free time to play and enjoy in the snow. Some of us visited the Ice Cave to enjoy playing with snowballs by making them as large as possible and then rolling them down the slopes. While others among us had moved inside the covered building, which had plenty of sitting space. The building was centrally heated, having many coffee and ice-cream parlors, flanked by the numerous shops selling trinkets and other attractive items. There were many restaurants each catering to the taste buds of a particular nation. There were many restaurants serving continental food. We had a look-around and then just relax sitting near the room heater at the glass paneled windows sipping coffee with a few of the elderly lot in our group. After sharing our personal experiences at this exciting place and sharing some eatables, we moved closer to the paneled windows to get a better viewing of the picturesque panorama that lay around us. Then we both moved around in the cold for quite a while seeing the winter sports lover gliding down hills or doing a superb, many twists, turns and jumps from the snow clad mountains. We began to feel the strain so decided to relax a bit along with many other elderly people of our group.

At the Terrace on top of the Mt. Titlis summit station, weather permitted, and many younger couples took an unforgettable ride on the "Ice Flyer", an enclosed ski lift that travels only a few meters over the Titlis Glacier. Some in our group who feared the lift over the glacier played throwing snow balls at each other or taking a turn for a ride on an ice-sledge, while some were sitting on the sledge others pushing the sledge. We took many pictures of ourselves in the open at the terrace and while sitting in the comforts of a hall gossiping. We missed the opportunity to click a picture dressed in a Swiss Costume at the Nostalgic Photo studio which could have been a perfect family memento.

Photos taken on our trip to Mt. Titlis

## Our halt at the Health Resort

The two of us enjoyed eating some of the local mouthwatering Swiss confectionaries and chocolate. We were already too full to be able to enjoy the Indian lunch subsequently served to us. Then we moved back in one of the giant cable car to a Health Resort to find a large number of health conscious people skiing. There were parents teaching their young children the art of the sport. It was heartening to see parents with their children enjoying as a group as they were participating in their joint venture. Some of our team mates including my wife went through a grueling experience of a ride on a rubber tube speeding down a funnel on a snow clad hill feature. The climb back to the starting point was extremely exhausting for Swapna. She was puffing and fuming but finally shared the looks of a lifetime achievement. The tired lot among us sat on a raised cemented platform covered with snow, ski-boots and other skiing- apparatus hanging on the racks at one corner of the platform. We watched many enjoying in the snow for a while. Curiosity provoked me to walk up to the corner of the platform and inspect the skiing apparatus which were stacked on the racks. They were of different sizes, colors and descriptions, rather heavy I thought. A lady walked up and suggested that I try out her gear. She was willing to strap them on me. I smiled, thanked and politely declined her offer. She persisted; skiing is not so difficult under proper guidance. She then pointed at the young boys and girls skiing. I still declined with the excuse of my breathing problems due to the elevation. She caringly patted me on my shoulder and left. We finally returned by cable car to our base where Mario was waiting to carry us to Lucerne.

## Lucerne

Lucerne is one of the six most frequently visited cities in the World. On arrival, we walked through the streets with picturesque buildings around us. Stopped at the spacious crossroads to look around and to take note of the direction we were walking. Finally we reached the world famous Lion Monument. A sculpture of a Lion in a majestic lying position, with lances pierced through its body had been chiseled on the face of a limestone cliff, which symbolically epitomizes the bravery and loyalty of Swiss Guards. This fascinating story is about the battalion of Swiss guards, who were providing protection to the Swiss Princess married to the then King of France, during the French Revolution when she and her young children were in the trouble hit district of France and the revolting mob armed with spears, daggers, lances and a variety of fearsome farm implements had resolved to kill and destroy all that belonged of the tyrannous King Louis XIV of France. The revolting mob was so desperate that they laid a siege to the fortress housing the Swiss Princess which was protected gallantly by a company of the Swiss guards. All of the Swiss soldiers laid their lives fighting till the last soldier was brutally slaughtered. Such is the dedication of the Swiss soldiers. Today even though Switzerland dose-not has a regular army to guard its borders, their soldiering excellence is still being recognized by the world. As a mark of respect by the Pope, all the guards at the Vatican City are of Swiss origin, dressed in Swiss soldiering costumes worn during the French Revolution.

Lion Monument

We strolled across the Kappelbrulcke - the oldest covered wooden bridge in the world, originally built in 1333 over river Reuss, leading to the 17th Century Jesuit Church. We had free time to shop at Schwanenplatz for Swiss army knives, bought bags full of Swiss chocolates, watches, souvenirs, etc.

Keppelbrucke wooden bridge

We continued our stroll along the picturesque Reuss River, enjoyed the spectacles of their opera houses, churches, and many other places of amusements. The Swiss enjoy a decidedly liberal sex life. They are also highly caring parents and love all kinds of sporting activities. I was told that the majority of the Swiss people speak Italian in the north, French in the southwest region and German language through the rest of their country. Their currency is the Swiss Franc with almost identical evaluation with Euro. As in the rest of the Christian world, day-by-day their church-going activities are declining. But I was told they still carry tremendous respect for the church and their religion. I suppose they have realized the importance of the religious values rather than merely adhering to the spiritual customs. As a mark of respect, people would offer a silent prayer of thankfulness to their God, before and after taking their meals and, ask for His guidance and protection before the bedtime.

After the long walks, our next halt was at the Lucerne lake front. We got a gorgeous view of beautiful swans, some of them were smoothly crossing the serene water-face and others basking on the shore with occasional flutter of their wings or being engaged in a swan dance with its mate. I also enjoyed observing little children emptying their lunchbox to the waiting swans.

Having emptied their own lunchbox they would turn to their parents, politely lament with anxious eyes that the birds are still hungry. Their parents would gently say give only a little bit more to eat or else the birds will suffer from bad-tummy. The children would invariably agree to the parent's request. Finally we were moving on to our next destination. Mario drove us through the beautiful Rhine belt of Switzerland. We were to travel 60 km in the north northeast direction to Zurich Airport. On our way, we had dinner at a fascinating place and finally moved to spend the night in the marvelous Hotel Moevenpick at Zurich International Airport.

Lucerne lake front

This was to be the last night of our memorable stays in the comforts of Hotel Moevenpick at Zurich International Airport. I enjoyed every bit of our stay in Switzerland. The country enjoys one of the highest GDP in the world. They boast of running the best of banking systems in the world. They are one of the most competent manufacturers of the best watches and other consortium of sophisticated products, and at the same time produce the finest of art, traditional folklore, classical literatures and other cultural themes like running fabulous opera houses, orchestrating consortium of musical compositions that the world has ever heard of. They provide one of the most valued social security to its people. In the world of sports, they are not lagging behind with their football teams and winter sports activities at the Olympics. They had even produced the best of the soldiers. Swiss soldiers are still recognized as the bravest fighting men who have been granted the honor to guard the Roman Catholic citadel of the Vatican City. Yet, for the past two centuries and more Switzerland has not felt the need to have a large standing army to defend its motherland. Even though, this small landlocked nation is bordering with dynamically volatile countries like Italy, Austria, Liechtenstein, Germany and France; who in the past four centuries have rocked the world with violence. In the recent past, the people of Switzerland are not known to be frequent Church goers, but they happen to follow a Bible like code of conduct in their day-to-day lives.

# Schaffhausen

## Rhine Falls

After the routine headcount by Amit the vehicle finally moved. Mario merrily whistled and drove the 90km to Schaffhausen in Switzerland to show us the mighty Rhine Falls. The mighty river Rhine Falls is the largest waterfall in Europe but not as large in size and volume compared to many of the water falls in South India or for that matter in the rest of the world. Tourists prefer to travel to the Rhine Falls because of its accessibility, romantic setting in a gorge straddled between two prominent hill top on either side of the Rhine Falls. It is a spectacle to watch the large volumes of 50 meters water sheets descending down the cliff multiplying its force eventually to roar, rumble and crash 30 meters below with thunderous gurgles while oozing froth as the turbulent water-force strikes boulders and other obstacles on its downward course. Water vapor and mist create a memorable vista which can be watched from the innumerable viewing-points stretched along the river-line. The other attraction for the young daunting thrill lovers is the nerve-racking boat rides to a gigantic cliff like rock jutting out just beneath the turbulent fall; at this point the turbulent water bifurcates to either side to circumvent the cliff; the water-bodies again collide to form ferocious gigantic waves to merge so as to create whirlpools. It is a thrilling experience to see the boatman, while avoiding the whirlpools, maneuver his boat to the cliff. After the passengers had climbed the rock with the help of the rope-ladder, they spent a while on top of the cliff and again climbed down the same way to return to shore. There are also many exotic eating-places along the river Rhine offering a magnificent view of the fall. The additional attractions to those sites were the delicious Swiss chocolates and mouth-watering Swiss ice-creams. We also bought a few souvenirs for our friends. Finally, but reluctantly we were ushered to our bus for the remaining journey of the day. Soon we crossed the Swiss-German border check-post and travelled further 150km along the River Rhine into Germany to visit a Cuckoo Clock Factory at Drubba near Heidelberg where we had to learn the mysteries that lie within the Black Forest and Rhineland in Germany.

At the Rhine Falls in Switzerland

# GERMANY

## Along Rhine River Belt

After the grueling experiences in Switzerland, we continued our journey traversing along river Rhine. As we moved on, I saw some of the spectacular displays of flora and fauna of the Black Forest in Germany. The name Black Forest was coined because of the denseness of the dark green pine trees that cover the rugged foothills of the mountains straddling the fertile banks of the peacefully meandering river Rhine. Spring to autumn the region is covered with deep green pine trees interspersing by other foliages like the brush green/yellow shrubs. On the lower slopes of the hills lay the cultivated fields with cattle grazing at places. But, during the severe winter months the entire area is covered with thick layers of sparkling snow. A birds-eye view of the area during the winter season I was told is like viewing below many beautifully decorated cakes with their unimaginably designed icings on top. As the gusty winds would blow swaying the lofty pines, one would notice pockets of gaunt, wet, desolated but murky undergrowth that lay below. It is only during the severe winter months when gusty winds would rent the air would one realize how severed and harsh conditions one would have to withstand. From time immemorial this region has witnessed many bloody skirmishes between rival Germanic tribes. They fought for survival in these dark, dense forests and to gain possession of the fertile river belt, so as to gain control over the Rhine River trade. The Romans on occupation of this region escalated the differences between the native Germanic tribesmen and enjoyed their spoils. The Holy Roman Empire during their rule over the region had called the French people Galls tribe and the people of the adjoining region Germanic tribesmen. The Galls were better organized and generally prevailed over the rustic Germanic cultivators. Subsequently for many years this region was ruled by Austria followed by Holland, France and Prussia. Disturbances within the locals, tribal factions continued as the change in the ruling class enforced their religious dogmas on the common people. In the beginning of the 16th century, Martin Luther of France began to question the dictates of the Roman Catholic Church and initiated the Protestant Reformation which engulfed large segments of the Germanic people to be converting to the Protestant faith. The tussle between different religious cults of Christianity continued for many years resulting in apathy towards the ruled class. The region remained divided between the Roman Catholic and the Protestant Church culminating to the 30 years war from 1618-48 which was fought between the Austrian Roman Catholic rulers and the Protestant Lords of Germany.

At the time of the French Revolution in 1789, France had annexed the Rhineland of Germany from Prussia. Napoleon on his ventures to Prussia, and onward to Russia had ruled over this region. In 1862, on account of the pervading dispute over Germany between Austria and Prussia, the latter deployed Otto Von Bismarck to quell the controversy. Bismarck was respected and loved by the Germans for his sincere administrative, social, educational and industrial reforms, which he had adopted for the development of Germany. Otto Von Bismarck of Prussia consolidated the region into a Federation for the German people. This relentless effort of consolidating the German people into a nation earned Bismarck the title Father of the German Nation. The feudal lords of Germany gradually regained control due to pervading corruptions at high offices, followed by a failed attempt at the industrial revolution by the commoners. Finally, the despotic ruler Kaiser Wilhelm dismissed Otto Von Bismarck in 1890. Kaiser was a self-seeking ruler who was routed from Germany after the 1914-18 World War 1. It is pathetic to observe how from time immemorial each one of these armies took possession of the fertile Germanic land to gain control of this strategically vital river along its course to the North Sea.

Barges and ferryboats loaded with streams of people occasionally moving up or down the river. I admired the German people for their spirit that bind them to their tasks of redeveloping their land after the two total wars their forefathers had fought for their Fatherland. Today, the Black Forest consists of a network of many beautiful picnic spots and hiking tracks which lie stretched along the hills interwoven with beautiful cottages and camping sites for the outdoor lovers to enjoy and to reflect on their heritages. Our vehicle gently descended down the lush green meadows or cultivated fields reminding me of Germany's agricultural past, and the smoke rising in the distance reminded of the present day gigantic industrializations.

River Rhine originating from the melting Alpine mountain ranges of Switzerland and Austria has many a tales to tell of its harrowing passage as the river runs across many countries like Germany, France, Luxembourg and Belgium as it carves its route northwest to meet the North Sea at the alluvial fertile delta coast of the Netherlands. The river-belt had also witnessed many a gruesome battles between merciless rivals like the Galls, Vikings, Normans, Romans, and also in the medieval period and up to the middle of the last century. Even today the river transportation is the cheapest mode of conveyance of men and material across the Euro-trade nations. Journey from here on has been along the fertile Rhine Belt till we reached the river delta near Amsterdam in Netherland.

## Dubba in Black Forest

The distance from Schaffhausen in Switzerland to Dubba in Germany is about 120km by road. As we moved on we saw stretches of cultivation at the lower plains of the mountain. At places we saw yellow flower blooming on small shrubs. Maybe they were not flowered but the plant itself had yellowish leaves. But the most spectacular sights were the dark green pine forests looming across the horizon over the mountains. Our vehicle finally stopped at Dubba in the very heart of the dark forest. This place is also the home of the Cuckoo Clock and the mouth-watering Black Forest Cakes and pastries. The long drive was rewarding as we sighted an unusually large cuckoo-clock shapes cottage. Our legs developed cramps due to squatting on the long drive. We desperately needed to exert our limbs, and many of us were also hungry. As though in anticipation Amit had arranged hot Indian lunch served in a tented restaurant just beside our vehicle parking area. It was a meal to be remembered particularly for the cozy Indian hospitality of the restaurant staff. After the meal, we were given an enlightened workshop/ demonstration of designing and assembling various types of cuckoo clocks. After the demonstration, we were taken around the factory sales counters displaying hundreds of a variety of cuckoo clocks having prices ranging from a few Euros to many thousands of Euros per piece. We purchased what our pockets could permit.

The Cuckoo Clock face building housing Cuckoo Clock Factory

Before leaving Dubba, we entered the nearby restaurant serving delicious Black Forest Cakes and pastries. The foodies enjoyed the black forest confectionaries. Thereafter, sharp at 3 PM we witnessed a fascinating display of local folk-dance with accompanying music managed by the mechanically managed human size dolls whirling and swaying with the Rhythm of the orchestra built within the towering Cuckoo clock on the wall of the building which was in front of us. This was on the front-face of the same factory building which we had earlier entered having brick-colored gabled roof, windows, doors and a balcony jutting out, where the dance performance was taking place. Just below the performing balcony with windows was a large round clock face with its immense hour and minute arms moving in unison with time of the day and on the strike of every hour the doors, windows and the balcony above displays this ceremonial performance. This was a spectacle which for a long time will remain fresh in my memory.

The vehicle moved on from Drubba towards Heidelberg, then flanking Frankfurt we moved beyond to Hokenheirn, a distance of approximately 100km. The day was filled with stressful activities. Finally at about 10.30 PM we huddled into the comforts of our room in Hotel Achat at Hokenheirn in the Rhineland of Germany.

We had to hurry through our morning rituals with little time to enjoy the sweet fragrance of our beautiful room, and yet I hastened to jot a word of appreciation for the comforts of the room enjoyed for a night spent in Germany. The room was packed with all essential amenities which had made our living comfortable. After the usual continental breakfasts with a variety of German cuisine we moved out at 8 AM to be amiably greeted by Mario at the vehicle parking area to transport us to the Rhine valley for the commencement of our enchanting Rhine Cruise.

The lavish suit we occupied at Hokenheirn was a reflection of the German people, their ethos and self-pride. Their love and pride for their Fatherland is remarkable. Some of the people brand the Germans lowly for their boisterous, rough, whimsical and resentfully behaviors. Many have scorned the Germans for their fondness of their root beer. But I have always found the Germans to be exceedingly upright and honorable in their dealings. My uncle and a brother-in-law of mine, who had spent some years in Germany about two to three decades back and share my views on the integrity of the German people. This country even after being shattered to rubbles twice within the span of fifty years in the last century; the united Germany today is at the top of the world's economy ladder. The speed, accuracy, precision and the precise manner with which they have been able to organize their river and road communication system are itself a marvel for the rest of the world to take a lesson from. Their present-day emphasis being on industrial developments, they have not lagged in the field of agricultural growth, sports, education, scientific research works and in other avenues of life.

## Cruise on the River Rhine

Our Rhine river cruise ship went past the legendary Lorelet Rocks, and we saw the medieval castles atop riverside cliffs. Then we came across cultivated fields on the steep mountain slopes, probably these were the new area additions to the existing stretches to the freshly pruned grapes plantations which were also on the mountain slopes. On both side of the river, we could see quaint looking houses made of timber which were probably settlements of farmers or lumberjacks. Our cruise was made particularly enjoyable because of the high spirit of the recently married couples. The younger couples of our tour team not only moved around from the deck to the barroom making friends and as well amusing us with fascinating stories they had picked up about a group from the Middle-east, who were said to be screaming and jostling within their group and seeking solace from the neutral observers standing nearby. Whosoever they were, nobody was interested in interacting with them.

As we sat comfortably enjoying the scenic beauty around us, some of our younger couples requested us to join them at the bar. At the bar, they all were in a carefree mood and were freely tasting different variety of German root beer, ice-cream and chocolates which they guaranteed were of a fine taste. The younger lots were requesting the elderly couples to join them in the merrymaking. For reasons unknown to me; the youngsters in our group were in a happy-go-lucky boisterous mood but certainly not a nuisance to the remaining sober people present at the bar. Finally, a young couple from our group, Surojit and Archana came up to us with two large cones of chocolate ice-cream and only then did we learn that it was their first marriage anniversary which they were celebrating on the cruise. We all wished them happiness, prosperity and a long life of togetherness.

Some Medieval Castles we saw on our way to
the ferry point for Rhine River Cruise

I thoroughly enjoyed the company of our young group, who too finally settled down admiring the landscape on either side of our moving cruiser. Many on board appeared to be regular traveler on this route and could name the hamlets and townships and the medieval fortresses we were crossing. An English speaking German noticing our interests and willingly narrated some intriguing historical facts of the region and kept us quite amused with some of the weird facts, customs and traits of the local folks.

We were thoroughly enjoying the company of the people around us when, Amit was the spoil-sport who beckoned us to assemble at the disembarkation point. We shook hands, exchanged a thankful glance and waved good-by to those who had shared our company, and we all moved to join the other members of our team at the disembarkation point. Thus, ended one of the many amusing part of this days visit to Europe.

Some of our memorable photographs on Rhine River Cruise

## Road to Cologne

The next part of our trip to commence soon was the fascinating two hours ride through the fertile middle Rhineland to Cologne in Germany. After disembarking; we continued a 120km journey by road to Cologne. The country side was picturesque. We noticed well paved roadways crisscrossing the mighty river Rhine and many unique sites of elevated broad water-channels crossings above another such water-channel. These water-channels carried cargo and other vessels across the length of Germany, and to neighboring countries. Water transportation is said to be a cheaper mode of conveyance than by land or air. I wondered whether similar thoughts are in the minds of the infrastructure developers in India since we are fortunately blessed with many rivers flowing down to the seas carrying sufficient volumes of water while flowing down through our country. We appreciated the progress made by Germany in various fields of development. We marveled the designs of the bridges we crossed, and appreciated the architectural skills of the buildings. I was enjoying watching the recently constructed buildings which gave a clean modern look to the scenic surroundings. It is evident that a new Germany has emerged from the country which was shattered to rubble 65 years ago by the advancing Allied Forces. My mind goes back to the sequence of events after the two dominant wars leading to the occupation of Germany by the four main Allied Forces of US, UK, France and USSR, so as to provide a security umbrella and assist the tottering Germany to rebuild its economy including all its core resources; so as to enable the victimized German people, once more to emerge as a new nation. Whereas USSR did little to help in rebuilding East Germany, but West Germany prospered under the NATO supervision.

## Cologne

At Cologne we had a hearty meal in an Indian restaurant named Rangoli. Finally, we were going in smaller groups to the shopping areas obviously for the ladies to purchase attractive mementoes. We were not able to get into any conversation with the local people as they only nodded to our queries and replied in German with a word or two sounding like English. However, they were expert in giving us directions in sign language. They locals were generally polite and replied in monosyllables, but never-the-less anxious and interested in helping foreign tourists. The most amusing part of our shopping was the purchase of eau-de-cologne which is recognized to be among the best body deodorant in the world. The shops also sold scrumptious chocolates and fabulous ice-creams. We were glad to purchase the original eau-de-cologne and to taste a large variety of chocolates.

A word about our bargaining power, I finally managed to impress my wife that I have a fantastic business sense. The incident was like this: we were purchasing some eau-de-cologne at a retail shop. We hackled with each other while selecting the perfumes from the samples. Even before, we could make up our mind for our final selection out of the items placed before us; the salesgirl attending us had jotted down the sample codes, neatly packed all of the eau-de-cologne which we had asked to be shown so as to make our final selections. The pretty salesgirl smiled and handed a slip of paper in my hand to be shown at one of the counters. The slip happened to be the cash-memo which I had submitted at the cash counter. The lady at the counter quickly handed me a bill and prompted the cash amount. I was surprised to receive a large amount on the bill handed to me for payment. I was stupid but paid the amount in cash to the lady sitting at the cash counter and proceeded to collect my package. The elderly lady at the cash-counter looked up at the two of us and asked what our problem was. Swapna blurted out my mistake. The lady was finally smiling and spoke in sugar-coated English, Sir, as an unusual case I have now charged your goods with an additional 30 percent festive discount. So, here is the refund amount, and this is your adjusted bills. You may produce the goods and the bills at the customs office at the International border check-post to claim further discount for your entitled duty exemptions. She smiled again and said, have an enjoyable trip in Germany. I thanked her and quickly put the coins in my pocket and moved out from the cash-counter without a second word.

During our travels in Europe, I had noticed that the locals preferred cycling. The use of centralized transportation like the trams and local trains were also preferred over the use of private cars. I was not surprised to find a few cycle-rickshaws and old fashioned buggy-carts on the road side. People were seen busy commuting to their place of duty. They seemed relaxed at the shopping arcades or at the open-air restaurants. They wore lighter shades of pure cotton dresses.

A few more customs which I heard the Germans follow filled my heart with admiration for their sense of responsibility. You may buy any amount of eatables at a restaurant but will have to consume all of it. Should you waste any food you shall be charged heavily for the food wasted and your entire party shall have to clean the dishes used at your table. Germans are highly conscious of millions of people in this world who do not get their daily bread. So, food cannot be allowed to be wasted. On the subject of daily food wastages; statistics revealed that daily food wastage in North America and Europe combined is enough to feed the undernourished children of Ethiopia for that day.

# Cologne Cathedral

Cologne located at the banks of river Rhine is a historic town in Germany. This place had played a significant role during WWII. This town is commonly referred by the Germans as Koln. This place is known worldwide for the gigantic Cologne Cathedral. This 515 foot tall gothic Cathedral took almost 6 centuries to build and the structure has the capacity to hold up to 40,000 people and is Germany's most visited monument.

The ancient site of Cologne Cathedral was a Roman Temple. From $4^{th}$ century, the site was occupied by Christian builders. A free standing baptistery was built in $6^{th}$ century. The baptistery was demolished in the $9^{th}$ century. At the same spot, a Cathedral was built which was completed in 818. It burnt down, and a new construction began at the same place in 1248 which was finally completed in 1880. During WWII, some damages took place to the Cathedral due to the Allied bombing which had shattered to rubble the remaining township of Cologne. In 1945 mindless American troops were said to have used the cathedral as a rifle range. The repair work to this world reckoned cathedral was finally completed in 1956.

After the morning briefing by Amit, we started a fascinating sightseeing adventure in which I have narrated tales of this mysterious city. The local people are not well conversant in English but cared to look concerned and ready to offer help. Our obvious first target was the awe imposing Cathedral. Though we visited this place first after our lunch at Rangoli, but I have decided to describe this place at the end. We took lots of photographs of the Cathedral from a distance, gradually we moved closer and finally inside the gigantic hall with the high alter the size of which I had never seen before. The photographs taken by me will bear evidence to the architectural excellence and the marvelous work of art left behind by the geniuses who had toiled to leave behind their creations within the four walls of this majestic Cathedral. There were many sculptures, murals, paintings and carvings on the stained glass window panels. I had ventured to photograph from different angles, from a distance for the total effect and then moved closer, and finally we stepped inside the vast congregation hall for detail effects. It was here when I felt the need for a better camera and a photographer friend by my side. From the very start, I was certain that I would not be able to describe the magnitude of this Cathedral to any of my friends in any language or words best known to me. A professional photographer could have helped me at this time.

At the appointed time and place we enter our coach to proceed to Belgium. On our way to the German-Belgium border I could see many stretches of lush green cultivated fields and herds of cattle grazing in pens. We had also come across some short stretches of dark green pine trees on the low lie of the hills. Then we saw many undulating meadows with natty hutments and barns at the edges of the fields. In the far distance almost at the skyline we could see at some places thin filters of smoke in the distance horizon, indicating some sort of industrial area, obviously catering to the international pollution norms.

Our vehicle moved along the luscious green fields of Germany for some time, then crossing the international border to Belgium where, a routine document checking of each passenger was carried out by the customs officials. We moved on, but there appeared no significant change in the topography except that the river Rhine was no longer giving us company for the next 3 hours of our journey. We travelled 160km to reach Antwerp in Belgium.

# BELGIUM

## Antwerp

Antwerp is a crucial seaport in Belgium. We reached this township at around 8 PM. The sun was still on the western horizon percolating a rich golden glow on the imposing buildings and the castles standing out as the citadel to the majestically laid out township. Our bus moved on the broad roads crossing to the boulevards and entered the avenues leading to the centre of the city. At times while turning on the crossroads we would get a whiff of fresh air from the North Sea and on occasions could see the masts of sailing ships and the giant cranes jutting out above the distant warehouses. There was not a soul in the broad roads and the streets we crossed were almost empty. But, as we turned on to an opening with a large fountain in the centre I had finally noticed a few stragglers on the streets who were casually going around as though they were enjoying a holiday. The roads in Antwerp were fairly broad and the buildings stately. We had gone past a few fortresses, while a castle we passed looked imposing. We also went past many strikingly prominent buildings and a few churches and maybe one or more palatial buildings indicating economic prosperity of the people living there. While moving past the well laid out metro city, we had to negotiate a few bridges over canals, but I could see only a few people on the roads, despite Antwerp being a large business centre of the European Common Market. This city also enjoys the second largest seaport in Europe and is said to be densely populated and carries a nasty reputation of being the most polluted city of Europe. Antwerp is also the largest diamond trading centre in the world. Then, where have the people gone? I was searching for an answer and yet reluctant to share my ignorance with the rest in our crowd. I remembered that since WWII a large Jewish community has dominated

Antwerp diamond trading industry, although the last two decades have seen Indian traders becoming increasingly influential. But, where have the people gone? Finally, it dawned on me that this day is Sunday the 24 of April 2011. Therefore, most of the people in the city were resting in their home and perhaps preparing for their busy schedule of the coming week. Eureka! This was obviously the reason. Realizing my stupidity, I laughed out loud for several seconds. Ultimately the vehicle stopped on the portico of Hotel Leonardo. We trickled drowsily out of the bus with our baggage in our hands. We were all obviously darned tired after the hectic activities of the day so we quietly entered hotel Leonard located in the very centre of the city. The hotel was not particularly prominent to look at but was surrounded by all the commercial buildings near at hand. We could hear whispers among the business community in our group exchanging references of jewel shops and diamond centers. We shall be returning to hotel Leonardo, to the same room for our next night's rest before proceeding to Brussels.

Some of the buildings we went past at Antwerp

Last night I had an unusually sound sleep. The wakeup call brought me back to the pragmatic realities of life. So, after a quick shave, shower and changing into the brightest color of casual wear I could think of, I smartly sauntered to our breakfast table and then to the reception-counter to hand over the keys fur room and proceeded accompanied by my wife to the waiting bus to be amiably greeted by Mario for a pleasant ride to the tulip gardens. Interestingly, a few of the business minded people on our trip complained of ill health and failed to turn up for the days outing to Netherland.

## History of the Netherlands

The history of the Netherlands is the history of the seafaring people thriving on a watery lowland river delta across the North Sea in North West Europe. The Romans arrived to this land in 57 BC. Then, the country was sparsely populated by tribal groups who generally lived at the periphery of the empire. Over four centuries of Roman rule had profound demographic effects, resulting eventually in the establishment of three primarily Germanic tribes in the area: Frisians, Low Saxons and the Franks. By the 8th century Hiberno-Scottish and Anglo-Saxon missionaries led them to adopt Christianity. The descendants of the Salian Franks eventually came to dominate the area, and from their speech the Dutch language arose.

Carolingian rule loosely integrated these tribes into the Holy Roman Empire, so the Viking depredation followed. The local noblemen were being left relatively free to carve out their highly independent duchies and counties. For several centuries, the neighboring clans fought intermittently amongst themselves, but at the same time trade continued and grew, land was reclaimed, and cities prospered. Forced by nature to work together, over the centuries they built and maintained a network of dikes that kept out the sea and floods, in the process transforming their desolate landscape, mastering the North Sea and the high seas beyond, and emerging out of the struggle as one of the most urban and enterprising nations in Europe.

By 1433, as a result of the defeat of the last countess of Holland the Duke of Burgundy had assumed control over most of the Dutch-speaking territories and the concept of a nation of Dutch-speaking people was conceived. Eventually, Burgundian Netherlands became a part of the Habsburg Empire and was ruled from Spain. With the passage of time a desire for reformation inflamed passions in the Dutch speaking people. In 1566 William of Orange, who is claimed to be the father of the Dutch clans, started the Eighty years' War to liberate the Dutch from the Catholic Spaniards brutality. The Dutch Republic was born, a nation with Protestants, Catholics and Jews and an unusual policy of tolerance. However, the southern provinces (present day Belgium) remained under Habsburg rule.

During this struggle, commerce continued to prosper. Amsterdam became the most powerful trading centre in northern Europe. In the Dutch Golden Age, which had its zenith in 1667, there was a remarkable flowering of trade, industry (especially shipbuilding), the arts (especially painting) and the sciences. The Dutch Republic, particularly Holland and Zeeland became a veritable Dutch empire and as a maritime power with a commercial, imperial and colonial reach that extended to Asia, Africa and the Americas – but not without slavery and colonial oppression. An interesting aspect of the Dutch people goes back to the start of the 18th century when their successive Royal Queens traditionally celebrates their birthdays on the 30th of April each year, an occasion when all the citizens of the Netherlands would don their national dress, which is in yellow color. This day being their national holiday draws out the spirit of the Dutch people, their love for their Queen and pride in their cultural heritages. This day is memorable for all Dutch nationals to have fun and enjoyments. All shops, offices and business are, closed for the day and movements on many roads are restricted. We were lucky to reach the Netherlands on the 25th of April and could move around freely as the restrictions of movements on roads were not yet affected. Another riveting fact is the Dutch economy pattern and her duty free trade with the nations of European Union. Almost all the nations of EU generally grow large varieties of flowers, fruits, live plants and products of floriculture including a large variety of dairy products of which Netherland alone exports around Euro 1.6 billion worth of these farm products to countries outside European Union like Switzerland, Russia, USA, Norway and Japan. Thus, the song, 'Tulips in the springtime and apples by the falls ……' perhaps had originated in this beautiful land.

# NETHERLAND

## Move to Keukenhof Gardens

I was very keen to see the magnificent Keukenhif Gardens as I have hears so much about the magnificent splendors that ate attached to that place. Our journey to the tulip garden appeared to me to be a never-ending ride to eternity. The two hours ride along the fertile alluvial plains of river Scheldt near Antwerp was something to remember as we were crossed the streets of Antwerp. We were one by one leaving behind those stately constructed of the present and the past era. I presumed that they were probably the office buildings, sprawling commercial places and finally the suburban buildings for schools, community centers and living accommodation. Living those far behind we were going past the rows after rows of white windmills with their huge blades going round and round with the breeze. We had finally reached into the heartland of Netherlands and was across the numerous Rhine deltas and finally to a place nearer to one of its estuaries of a river Impatient, as we all were, our vehicle continued to move on and on, bisecting stretches after stretches of ploughed fields, pens full of farm horses, then we saw cattle peacefully grazing and the numerous warehouses, farm-cottages, milk-factories and yet no sight of any tulips. Our bus moved on.

Finally, at far-off distances we could see stretches after stretches of tulip cultivation with rows after rows of red, blue, purple, indigo, white and yellow colors. As we moved on, we crossed many more stretches of tulip cultivation at a closer distance. I was simply staring down at the rows after rows of colorfully cultivated tulip fields. Draped they were I saw in astounding colors of greens, reds, blues, yellows, purple and perhaps whitish-pink flowering beds. Before my eyes were the exquisite flowers in rows after rows of the most gorgeous colors appearing to have been weaved together to reach the distant horizon. The fields below the embankments of the swelling water front were the long, never-ending beds of flowers. Beyond the dykes, waves after waves of seagulls were lurching to a height, then diving down, swirling and swerving along the waterfront, then mysteriously disappearing behind the clouds. The sharp, shrill calls these birds were making resonated in my mind. It appeared to me as though the birds were crying for help or screaming a warning that a storm is near to come, but, dauntlessly Mario was moving us to our destination, which was the world famous Keukenhof Gardens in Netherland. We were told by our guide that, at this time of the year the tulips are said to be blooming at its best so we should see be able to see the splendor of this magnificent garden of flowers of exquisite varieties.

## Keukenhof Gardens

We were lucky to visit the Keukenhof Gardens during the famed National Flower Exhibition (open from mid April to mid May). This year we were a few out of the millions that journey to this garden every year at this momentous time. I was spellbound at the sight of the vivid displays of over seven million Tulips, Daffodils, Narcissi and other varieties of flowers, lakes and amusement areas spread over 80 acres of stunning landscape and thematic gardens. I feel there is no need to give any description of this garden any further since some of the photographs that I had taken of the Keukenhof Garden are shown below which adequately exhibit the exotic beauty of flowers and the imaginative laid out topography that mark this garden's spacious layout. We were extraordinarily lucky to be able to visit the Keukenhof Garden a day after its auspicious opening for the annual flower show exhibition attended by the world's florists once every year. This flower show ceremony is held just ahead of The Netherlands national holiday to celebrate the birthday of their dearest Queen, traditionally celebrated each year on the 30th of April. Since 1715, his regal occasion is celebrated throughout the Netherlands. The people of the Netherlands don their national color orange. The participants would be in a gay and frivolous mood, merrily participating in fanfare on the streets. They would totally immerse in traditional folk dances, singsongs, and watching the exquisite federal fire-displays. The entire township would be lit-up, whereas the people rejoice totally immersed in a general spirit of merrymaking.

Our pictures from the Keukenhof Gardens

## The Cheese Factory

We left the Kaukonof Garden at 1PM to board the waiting bus. Fragrance of the multitude of flowers we had seen in the picturesque layout still lingered in my mind. As we were moving towards Hague, the political capital of The Netherlands I was experiencing satisfaction and the fulfillment of a dream. Soon, we were moving for a quick lunch at a makeshift eating place at a cheese factory warehouse. Our lunch was brought to us by a catering-van. With the taste of Indian curry still lingering we leisurely walked across to yet another residential cottage complex which was exhaling many a variety of mouthwatering aromas of "Gau Mata Cheese" and Dutch chocolates. Before entering the cheese factory, we enjoyed a small recess when we relaxed and took many photographs.

The technique of making Dutch vegetarian farmhouse cheese is an art of fermenting fresh, raw milk using traditional methods in wooden barrels. We were given an excellent demonstration on the sequences of making "Halal Cheese". Some of us including Swapna voluntarily participated in the demonstration. After the demonstration, most of us availed the opportunity of testing the sample cheese of various vintages and enjoyed the chocolates which were being lavishly distributed among the customers. Of course, we too bought a lot of the local stuff.

As I am dwelling on this subject of manufacturing cottage cheese I would like to mention that many a different varieties of cheese are manufactured in different parts of Europe with different preparation processes and flavors, meant to be eaten at different occasions. The best of the foreign cheese which are popular in Indian are the Swiss cheese, Italian mozzarella and the Dutch Halal Cheese with many variations of vegetarian (organic) Gou Mata Cheese. So as to distinguish the differences in their flavors we were offered almost all of the above varieties. Indeed a crackerjack sales technique where-by the other cheese manufacturing groups were the willing participants.

At the Cheese Factory

# Dykes of Holland

Most of the land in the northern part of Holland which is now called The Netherlands is reclaimed marsh land, once submerged at high tide or were flooded due to the frequent storms at sea. Over the centuries, even before the mediaeval period, these low lying alluvial delta land had been reclaimed by building ramps (dykes/dams). The Netherlands and the greater part of Belgium that we know of today are the reclaimed land from the North Sea by the use of dykes. The man made water channels are extensively used for the cultivations and other human necessities by channelizing the entry of salt water from the North Sea by building networks of dykes with sluice gates. Then at the filtering plants the saline water is processed for human consumption and irrigation purposes. The industrial wastes are also processed before recycling the water for reuse. The excess of water is drained out to the North Sea by maintaining strict control on the operation of the sluice gates, designed to control the flow of water to various areas within the matrix of the dykes.

We climbed up the ramps of a few dykes and saw the sea level across the bund was well above the level of the cultivated land. The height of the dykes were generally 20ft to 25ft and, at certain places even higher above the general level of the land whereas the water levels at high tides was 10ft to 15ft above the reclaimed land mass. I am told that the people living in this part of the world are extremely hardy, God fearing, happy-go-lucky and accustomed to facing many a hazard particularly when the dykes were breached by the fury of high rising waves, resulting from the frequent hurricanes at North Sea as well as the Baltic Sea. Another intriguing point arising out of the Alpine mountain ranges in the south-central Europe from where the main rivers in Europe flow northward to the northern seas has resulted in the busiest seaports of Europe in the north like Amsterdam, Rotterdam and Antwerp which are the classical examples of cities that stand protected by the dykes. We had climbed up the ramps of a few of the dykes and observation posts.

## Wooden shoe at Ratterman's Factory

We moved from the Ratterman's Cheese Factory along the dykes to the Ratterman's Wooden shoe Factory. Wooden shoes have been popular in the Netherlands for about 700 years. Wooden shoe wearers claim the shoes are warm in winter, cold in summer and provide support for healthy posture. The wood also absorbs perspiration so that the foot can breathe. Wooden shoes, as icons of Dutch culture, appear in customs such as the practice of young Dutch men presenting their fiancés with a pair of carved wooden shoes. I somehow got an urge to do the same. The scene has been nicely photographed by one of our friends in the group. Another notable feature is that, in Holland, wooden shoes are worn to protect their feet from nails, fishing hooks and sharp implements that might pierce a regular boot, not wooden shoe. While working on boats, docks and in muddy fields, wooden shoes keep feet dry. Wooden shoes are also worn as an essential part of the traditional costume for Dutch clogging. Clogs for dancing are made differently so that they'll be lighter. The soles are made from ash wood, and the top part is cut lower by the ankle. Dancers create a rhythm by tapping the toes and heels on a wooden floor.

## Making of Wooden Shoes

We were lucky to witness a live demonstration of making a wooden shoe. The process appeared exceptionally clear where the machine did most of the work. The finer designing and the artistic shaping was done by a professional worker. Today, wooden shoes are mostly made by machine. There are not many wooden shoe makers left, but they can be found in some of Holland's tourist areas. These artisans demonstrate the many tools they use and how they select a tree trunk or log according to the size of shoe they are going to make. Both shoes of a pair must be made from the same kind of wood, even the same side of a tree, so that the wood will shrink at the same rate. Usually, sycamore, alder, willow and poplar woods are used for handmade clogs, and birch is used for machine-made. Clogs made in Holland must pass certain tests that measure how they endure extreme temperatures and heavy weight.

At the end of the amusingly conducted demonstration, we moved over to the sales department and saw some of the unique varieties of the Clog shoes. Finally, we moved out to see a few of the preserved windmills of the medieval period. Thereon we moved to Amsterdam.

We followed the Dutch traditions

Windmills - a symbol of the Netherlands

# Amsterdam

## History of Amsterdam

Before our Europe tour, I did not know much about the history of Amsterdam but, after rambling in the main street and the market square I had learnt a lot. Subsequently, some of us moved to the canal cruise embarkation point for an orientation tour along the extensive canal network of city. So, some of us particularly the senior lots boarded a cruiser while a few of the energetic couples ventured deeper into the city with Amit, their perennial guide. However, we had the mutual understanding of sharing notes on returning to the place of our rendezvous.

As the boat kept moving, the announcer on board after welcoming the passengers, briefly indicated the prominent landmarks on shore, and he continued narrating the history of Amsterdam. His demeanor was as though none other dare to reveal the secrets of this ancient city. I was thoroughly impressed and recorded his speech.

The origins of the city of Amsterdam lay in the 13th century, when the fishermen living along the banks of the River Amstel built a bridge across the waterway near a large saltwater inlet. Wooden doors on the bridge served as a dam; these protected the town from the sea which often flooded the early settlement. The mouth of the river Amstel, where the Demark now is, formed a natural harbor, which became necessary for trade. Around 1275 this region came under Holland and was named Wasteland. As a special favor for the use of their fishing boats the fishermen of Wasteland region had the right to travel through the country of Holland without having to pay toll. In subsequent years its name had developed into Amsterdam. According to legend, on 12 March 1345, the miracle of Amsterdam occurred and Amsterdam became a prominent pilgrimage town. The town grew considerably, thanks to the pilgrims. A Roman Catholic procession occurs every year to celebrate the miracle. During the 14th and 15th century, Amsterdam increasingly acquired grain and timber, so became the granary of the northern low-countries and the most powerful trading city in Holland, which considerably strengthened the position of the city. Subsequently, contacts laid through the beer trade formed the basis for further trade with cities of the Baltic Sea. Two massive fires swept through the city in 1421 and 1452. After the second, where three quarters of the city were destroyed, Emperor Charles decreed that new houses were to be built from stone. Few wooden building is still remaining from this period.

The 16th century brought a rebellion by the Dutch against the Habsburg king of Spain and lead to the Dutch independence. The uprising was mainly caused by the lack of political power for the local nobility and by the religious intolerance of the Spanish. The people of Amsterdam began the war, but, on the Spanish side they changed sides in 1578 and gave their support to William I of Orange, leading to the Dutch independence. One of the results of the war was that Spanish religious intolerance gave way to Dutch tolerance. In Amsterdam people were free to believe what they wanted, but within certain limits. In the city, a large Roman Catholic minority remained. Roman Catholicism is still the major religions denomination in Amsterdam, but many people belonged to the Reformed Church and other Protestant denominations. During these years, religious wars raged throughout Europe and many people fled to the Dutch Republic and Amsterdam, where they sought refuge. Wealthy Jews from Spain and Portugal, prosperous merchants from Antwerp and the Huguenots from France all sought safety in Amsterdam.

The latter part of the 16th century to about the third quarter of the 17th century was Amsterdam's Golden Age. Prosperity prevailed. Ships from the city sailed to North America, Indonesia, Brazil and Africa and formed the basis of a worldwide trading network. Amsterdam's merchants financed expeditions to the four corners of the world, and they acquired the overseas possessions which formed the seeds of the later Dutch colonies. The city expanded enormously around its canals during this time. Amsterdam was the most pivotal point for the transshipment of goods in Europe, and it was the leading financial centre of the world (a position later taken over by London).

During the 17th and 18th century, Amsterdam was a city where immigrants formed the majority. Most immigrants were Lutheran-Protestant Germans. The enormous impact of German immigration can be seen nowadays in the surnames. The integration of immigrants was smooth. It was not hard to find work as a craftsman, but craftsmen were forced to join guilds, to serve in the city patrol and to cooperate to compete with other districts. These were powerful institutions that resulted in quick integration, especially since all these institutions were mainly filled with immigrants or children of immigrants. The city council of Amsterdam consisted out of people with all kinds of backgrounds: Dutch, German, Flemish, French and Scottish.

The 18th and early 19th centuries saw a decline in Amsterdam's prosperity. The wars of the Dutch Republic with the United Kingdom and France took their toll on Amsterdam. During the Napoleonic wars, Amsterdam's fortunes reached their lowest point; however, with the establishment of the Kingdom of the Netherlands in 1815, things slowly began to improve.

At the end of the 19th century, the Industrial Revolution reached Amsterdam. The Amsterdam-Rijn canal was dug to give Amsterdam a direct connection to the Rhine and the Noordzee canal to give the port a connection with the North Sea. Both projects improved communication with the rest of Europe and the world dramatically. They gave the economy a tremendous boost. The end of the 19th century is sometimes called Amsterdam's second Golden Age. New museums, the Central Station and buildings of cultural institutions and opera houses were built. Also, built was a unique ring of 42 forts and land that could be inundated to defend the city against an attack. Amsterdam's population grew significantly during this period. During World War I, the Netherlands remained neutral, but Amsterdam suffered the effects of the war when food became scarce. In 1932, a dike separating the Zuider Zee from the North Sea was completed. The new lake was made behind the dyke. For the first time, in its history Amsterdam had no open communication with the sea.

During World War II, German troops occupied the city. More than 100,000 Jews were deported, famously including Anne Frank, almost entirely wiping out the Jewish community. Before the war, Amsterdam was the world's centre for the diamond trade. Since this trade was mostly in the hands of Jewish businessmen and craftsmen, the diamond trade essentially disappeared.

The cultural revolution of the 1960s and 1970s made Amsterdam the magical centre of Europe. The use of soft drugs was tolerated, and this policy made the city a popular destination for hippies. Squatting became widespread. Riots and clashes with the police were frequent. A grim atmosphere took hold of Amsterdam. Anarchists, such as the Provost and a local political movement wanted to change the local society. The construction of the underground Metro under the oldest parts of the city also led to widespread protests due to the impact of the construction on heritage buildings and local residents. Amsterdam started the 1980s in an explosive manner. While Queen Beatrix's coronation was being held in the New Church on Dam square, protesters outside the church fought with the police in protest against government policies. Their slogan was 'No house, no coronation'. When the mayor feared the uprising was getting violent, he directed the military to get the situation under control.

During the 1970s, the number of foreign immigrants, primarily from Surinam, Turkey and Morocco grew strongly. This led to an exodus of the local peoples to other cities near Amsterdam. However, neighborhoods like the Pijp and the Jordaan, which had previously been working class became sought out places of residence for the newly wealthy and students. Amsterdam that used to be a poor city in the Netherlands turned into an economically rich city thanks to the new, economical trend towards a service-economy instead of an industrial economy.

At the beginning, of the millennium social problems such as safety, ethnic discrimination and segregation between religious and social groups began to develop. 45% of the population of Amsterdam has non-Dutch parents. Large social groups are people from Surinam, the Dutch Antilles, Morocco and Turkey.

## Cultural life at Amsterdam

In the 15th and 16th century, cultural life in Amsterdam consisted mainly of festivals. During the later part of the 16th century in Amsterdam, a Chamber of Rhetoric organized contests between different Chambers in the reading of poetry and drama. In 1638, Amsterdam got its first theatre. Ballet performances were given in this theatre as early as 1642. In the 18th century, French theatre became popular. Opera could be seen in Amsterdam from 1677; first only Italian and French operas, but in the 18th century German operas included. In the 19th century, popular cultural centers sprouted in an area in Amsterdam, mainly for vaudeville and musical. The metronome, one of the most fundamental advances in European classical music was invented here. With the 20th century came cinema, radio and television

Our meeting with those from our excursion group was exciting. I was beginning to regret not accompanying the budding youths of the excursion group. They had physically visited most of the historic places told to us by our announcer. What more, they had visited many of the cultural centers, the opera houses, fascinating museums including a sex museum, shopping arcades and many other intriguing places. Truly, Amit would have shied away from taking us, the elderly lot to some of the places where large, many immigrants from Africa, Middle-East, notorious Asians and those from Central America once had the hippy culture glowing. While discussing amongst our mutually selected groups and after the usual headcount by Amit, our luxury bus moved along the northern coast of The Netherlands till we neared Rotterdam.

Rambling on the streets of Amsterdam

Our canal cruise begins along the residential area

## Rotterdam

At this point, I would like to mention a few things about the city of Rotterdam. Like Amsterdam Rotterdam too has an identically long history. Rotterdam is the second-largest city in the Netherlands and one of the largest ports in the world. Starting as a dam constructed in 1270 on the Rotte River, Rotterdam has grown into a leading international commercial centre. Its strategic location at the Rhine-Meuse-Scheldt delta on the North Sea and at the heart of a massive rail, road, air and inland waterway distribution system extending throughout Europe are the reason that Rotterdam is often called the "Gateway to Europe". Rotterdam is one of Europe's most vibrant, multicultural cities; known for its university (Erasmus), cutting-edge architecture, lively cultural life, striking riverside setting, its maritime heritage and the Rotterdam Blitz. It has the largest port in Europe and one of the busiest ports in the world, the port of Rotterdam was the world's busiest port from 1962 to 2004, when it was surpassed by Shanghai. Rotterdam's commercial and strategic importance is based on its location near the mouth of the Nieuwe Maas, a channel in the delta formed by the Rhine and Meuse on the North Sea. These rivers lead directly into the centre of Europe, including the industrial Ruhr region. Rotterdam is currently bidding to host the 2018 Summer Youth Olympics. Leaving Rotterdam to our north, we moved along the meadows till we had reached Antwerp in Belgium, for a well deserved night's stay at our hotel Leonardo.

# BACK TO BELGIUM

## Brussels

### History of Brussels

Before the day's excursion a brief history is a must. Brussels in Old Dutch means marsh or "home in the marsh". The settlement that was to become Brussels was once a chapel on an island in the river Senne around the year 580 AD. The bishop of Cambrai made the first recorded reference to the place "Brosella" in 695 when it was still a hamlet, because of its location on the shores of river Senne on a vital trade route between Bruges and Cologne. Brussels grew quite quickly as a commercial centre and rapidly extended towards the upper town where there was a smaller risk of floods. As it grew, the surrounding marshes were drained to allow for further expansion. After the construction, of the first walls of Brussels in the early 13th century Brussels grew. In-between 1356 and 1383 the city expanded and The Grand Place was gradually developed along with a second set of walls erected. Today, traces of it can still be seen mostly because the "small ring", a series of roadways in downtown Brussels bounding the old historic city centre.

As a result of a long lasting conflict with France, in 1695, the King Louis VIII of France sent troops to bombard Brussels with artillery, which even destroyed the Grand Place along with many thousands of buildings and a third of the city. The reconstruction of the city centre was carried out during the subsequent years which profoundly changed the appearance of the city and left numerous traces of demolition still visible today. The city was subsequently captured by France in 1746 during the War of the Austrian succession, but was handed back to Austria three years later.

Brussels remained with Austria until 1795, then with Southern Netherlands till captured and annexed by France. Brussels became the capital, and it remained as a part of France until 1815, when it joined the United Kingdom of the Netherlands.

In 1830, the Belgian revolution took place in Brussels and became the capital and seat of government of the new nation. In 1831, Leopold I, the first King of the Belgians, ascended the throne. He undertook the destruction of the city walls and the construction of many buildings. Following independence, the city underwent many more changes. River Senne had become a serious health hazard, and from 1867 to 1871 its entire course through the urban area was thoroughly covered over. This allowed urban renewal and the construction of modern buildings and boulevards characteristic of downtown Brussels today. Throughout this time, most parts of Brussels remained a Dutch-speaking city, though until 1921 French was the sole language of administration. However, in 1921, Belgium was formally split into three language regions—Dutch-speaking Flanders, French-speaking Wallonia and bilingual Brussels. During World War I, German troops occupied the city of Brussels but did not incur much damage. In World War II, the city was again occupied, and was spared serious damage during its occupation by German forces before it was liberated by the British.

## Orientation Tour of Brussels

After a continental breakfast, we checked out of our hotel and drove towards Brussels. On arrival we proceeded for an orientation tour. It is often said that Brussels is best viewed on foot, particularly the old city, which as I have mentioned earlier, was constructed and reconstructed between 13th to 18th century, where most of the roads are narrow and winding along the magnificent structures and some of the beautiful monuments give an impression of having been reconstructed. The later addition, the new city is undoubtedly open, spacious, but the buildings are haphazardly built.

# The Old Brussels

After narrating the torments and the ravages faced by the natives of Brussels in the historic past, the Grand Place still exists at the central square of the Grote Market at Brussels. This marvelous piece of architect still continues to be surrounded by pictorial Guildhalls, the city's Town Hall, and the Kings 'Breadhouse'. The square is the most prominent tourist destination and most memorable landmark in Brussels and it is a UNESCO World Heritage site. After a long days walk in the streets of Brussels I enjoyed seeing the picturesque surroundings of the Grand Place market square at the Grote Market. We did not have the time to venture inside those forbearing buildings, which on the exterior are amply garnered with exquisite sculptures and awesome designs. As we moved, we could see the gigantic St. Michaels church in the distance. We continued to ramble further down the winding lanes on the east flank of the square to reach a breath taking spot where lay on the wall, a lady in brass, in an awe inspiring tranquil state. The serine statue if you touch after offering a prayer to the divine lady, one shall have his wishes fulfilled. We not only marveled the unique sculpture but simply revered the saintly figure, but also touched and offered a prayer. Thereafter, we moved beyond to the Manneken Pis Statue, where stands the sculpture of an infant boy standing in a posture to pee. The little boy was lost for five days, and his anxious parents finally found him mindlessly standing at that very same spot and exactly that same posture. This incident is said to have happened many centuries ago, and the then monarch of Brussels had declared that a statue be erected at the spot to commemorate the return of the lost child. Such were the humor enjoyed by the simple Belgians. Among other attractions were the rows after tows of shops displaying local garments, and many attractive items inclusive of the delicious Belgium ice cream, and many shops were displaying many mouthwatering confectionaries. Finally, we rambled back to the Grote Market, where among other attractions we feasted our eyes on the beautiful flowers and decorative saplings which were for sale at exorbitantly high price for our pocket. Never-the-less we enjoyed seeing the exquisite displays and finally moved out of the city for our onward journey to the new city area.

## The Brussels Town Hall

## The New Brussels

New Brussels was developed after the two Great Wars of 20th century. Even though not many damages had occurred to the buildings during the World Wars, yet Brussels was being modernized for the European Union. Many new constructions were being built by unnecessarily demolishing the old buildings of historic importance to make way for the new constructions. Many of the demolished areas are still lying vacant. The construction of the North–South connection linking the main railway stations in the city was completed in 1952. Many of the grand structures that have come up were the superbly new Grand Place which is housing the seat of the Republic of Belgium. There is the new museum and the new library considered to be containing the finest collection of reading material that ever was. As a symbol of modernization Atomium structures are in abundance all over Brussels. Some of the new buildings look formidable and very impressive to look at. There are plentiful places for amusements and the sports lovers have easy access to their sports activities. Starting from the early 1960s, Brussels became the de facto capital of what would become the European Union, and many modern buildings were built. Unfortunately, development was allowed to proceed with little regard to the aesthetics of newer buildings, and many architectural gems were demolished to make way for newer buildings that often clashed with their surroundings. This process was known as Brusselization. The Brussels-Capital Region was formed after a constitutional reform in 1988. It has bilingual status, and it is one of the three federal regions of Belgium, along with Flanders and Wallonia.

As we were moving past many of the streets and lanes of the Capital Region of Brussels, Amit was indicating the important landmarks, till we reached the three most conspicuous structures of the modern age Brussels, the new Grand Palace flanked by a gigantic building housing the library, and the third prominent structure was Atomium, situated diagonally opposite the other two structures. It was here that we had some free time to move around on our own and enjoyed taking photographs' of ourselves. As time was at premium, we had to be in time for our evening sessions at Paris. So, as we moved on, we crossed the lush green and yellow fields and were leaving the rows after rows of white windmills fading away in the distance, till finally reaching the Belgian-France border check-post. Our journey from Brussels to Paris was well over 200km.

Atomium

## Brussels to Paris

After our six hours of grueling experiences in Brussels, our journey from Brussels to Paris was completed in about two hour time. After crossing the border outpost we could see significant changes in the panorama around us. I noticed a distinctively better layout of the cultivated fields, remarkably larger and greater number of industrialized places. The buildings bore a colorfully modern grandeur. Hopefully we were nearing Paris, the fashion capital of the world.

# FRANCE

Mario moved on, pressing the throttle of his bus to the maximum permissible limits. Gaily we moved on, sharing with friends many of our experiences in Europe. Two of our jovial tourist narrated a funny experience they had with a German, a cab driver at Cologne. They were trying to impress a German cabdriver by an effort to speak in German language, to take them to a restaurant to buy beer. Their best of efforts did not make any sense to the cabdriver. Then they tried in English, again no results, he only gave a blank look. The two them got disgusted and lost their patience. In disgust and anger some filthy remarks was made in Hindi about that German people and the cabdriver in particular. That hefty German fellow jumped out of his cab and angrily pelted bursts of the choicest abuses in Hindi. The two of them were confused and flabbergasted. Finally, the German grinned, and spoke in fluent English. He explained that, if you don't know German language then why do you want to murder my sweet father tongue. As he took us to the restaurant he explained that long back he was at Bombay for two years and had learnt only to speak the foulest of abuses in Hindi and Marathi. Many others joined in with their treasured experiences in foreign lands. Our bus moved on. Ladies, as usual settled down to talking about their purchases of exotic goods. I was busy recollecting the geography, history, the cultural and many other aspects of France; including the socio-economic developments of the region. I was preparing myself for a deeper understanding of this vast land and its people. Some consider it wasting ones valuable time to dwell on the background of the places, as we would get the updated story after reaching that place. I know that it is not possible to travel to each and every place of every tourist's interest. Therefore I am also including some of the other places of interest in my travel memoirs.

## Topography of France

After Russia, France is the second largest country in Europe. To its north is the Bay of Biscay and the English Channel separating Great Britain from France. To its south is the Mediterranean Sea. On its west is Spain and its east is flanked by Belgium, Germany, Switzerland and north-west Italy. The Pyrenees Mountain ranges divides Spain from France, where as its southern region is bound by a range of mountains from where river Seine and Loire flow northward to the English Channel and the Bay of Biscay respectively, whereas river Rhone flows southward to the Mediterranean.

## Brief History of France

Stone tools discovered in 2009 indicate that early man was present in France at least 1.57 million years ago. It is bereaved that around 600 BC the Greeks had founded Marseilles at the shores of the Mediterranean Sea and the city is believed to be the oldest city in the world. In some historic records there are mentions of the existence of a number of tribes living in the present territory of France. Some of the Gallic Celtic tribes penetrated into some parts of France. Historical records indicate that from 5th BC to 3rd BC the same Gallic Celtic expanded their regime and finally, had occupied the rest of France including present day Belgium, north west portion of Germany and some parts of north west Italy. The Roman brought with them some warlike tribesmen who defeated the Galls. Later the Carthaginian commander Hannibal with the help of Gaul mercenaries' soldiers defeated the Romans. The pride of the Gauls was once more restores in many parts of France. In later years Julius Ceaser with his Roman Gaul forces conquered the rest of Gaul in the Gallic Wars of 58 to 51 BC. In due course of time a Gallic-Roman culture increasingly integrated into the Roman Empire. The Gauls remained under Roman control and Celtic culture was gradually being replaced by Gallo-Roman culture. In the years that followed Barbarian tribes were constantly migrating into the Gallo-Roman territories in France and were being called by the name of Germanic Franks. The Frankish King Clovis I united most of Gaul under its rule in the late 5th century, setting the stage for Frankish dominance in the region for hundreds of years. Frankish power had reached its glorious period under Charlemagne. Over the years that followed, the medieval Kingdome of France achieved their increasing prominence under the rule of the House of Capet founded by Hugh Capet in 987 AD. Following the death of the last Capatin monarch in 1337, led to a series of conflicts known as the Hundred Years war. Finally the Hundred Years War of religious dominance ended with a Valois victory in 1453. During the next centuries, France experienced the Renaissance and religious reforms by the Protestant faith. In the 16th century France along the European world was moving with other powers as a worldwide colonial power.

In the late 18th century most of the other countries in Europe was facing industrial unrest whereas France was in the grip of the French revolution. The monarchy and associated institutions were overthrown in theFrench Revolution. That ultimately resulted in the change of course of the French and the world history. France was ruled by a Republic government until the French Empire was declared by Napoleon Bonapate. Following Napoleon's defeat at the Battle of Waterloo he was exiled for life at the Island of St Helena. France went through several further regime changes, being ruled as a monarch, then briefly as a second Republic and again a period of rule by an Emperor followed by third Republic and finally the French government stabilized in 1870. During the WW I, France was a member of the Triple Entent power and fighting alongside the United Kingdom, Russia and their allies and were fighting the Central Powers of Germany and its allies. Whereas During the WW II, France was conquered by Nazi Germany within two months. After the war in 1945 the Fourth Republic and within a decade or so in 1958 the Fifth Republic of France into focus and is still functioning. Soon t the French colonial empires became independent, leaving a few which were merged into the French states as oversees establishment. Today France is a member of the UN, the UE and NETO and is culturally, economically and militarily strong with a politically stable government

# Paris

## Orientation tour of Paris

We were moving through the history of Paris, going back roughly 600 years before the 19th century. Major ruling dynasties from France, Austria and England have changed hands over Paris many a time, leaving behind dynamically vibrant edifice of monuments and cultural themes to this beautiful city. Among others, the 12th century Notre Dame Cathedral and many of the 17th century constructions by Louis XIV called the Sun King and other development trends, continued further during the Napoleonic era, and beyond till 20th centuries Eiffel Tower; they had pioneered the panoramic grandeurs of Paris, which till this day is marveled by all. Paris is regarded as the sister city to Rome. Amit was conducting our orientation tour of Paris for the day. Our orientation tour commenced from the northeastern suburb district of Paris. The metropolis of Paris is one of the most frequented tourist destination in the world. Paris is cosmopolitan in nature, where people from any and every part of the world have made their home. In the suburbs people of different demographic regions of the world prefer to live together, which later proved to be bothersome to the city administration, due to the foreign cultural and ethnic trends seeping into their socio-economic patterns in those localities. We saw the lofty mansions, broad roads, spacious walking paths, greeneries between the road dividers, and at the same time, we saw weekly bazaars as in many developing countries. These bargaining places are generally in the central pathways, and at places we saw well laid out fruits, vegetables and other grocery items being sold on the footpaths, as seen in many parts of Europe where beer, coffee, tea and eatables are served in the outdoor restaurants along the footpaths. Everything around seemed to move at a lazy space, giving a sense of fulfillment in the people that live there. Gradually we were moving into more organized districts, where people more frequently communicated in French. Some of these places were vibrating with a romantic touch of the culture and fashion usually associated with the people of France and their traditions. We came across many of the significantly important monuments that Paris is well known for. There was the Notre Dame Cathedral looking majestically large, whose construction began in 1163 and took two centuries to complete the masterpiece. Then saw the Town Hall, the fabulous building that housed the Mayor's office complex. Thereafter, we saw the miniature statue of liberty and many other fascinating sites which shall later be explained to us by an expert local guide. Now was the time for a quick late lunch.

Like in India there are weekly bazars for the needy

## Gala Evening in Paris

In the evening, we had in store for us a 'Gala Evening in Paris' that combines fun and entertainment. The Gala Evening included a glass of classic French wine, the finest and most dazzling combination of beauty, rhythm and gaiety at the Parades Latin Show. This Opera was built in 1889 and partially designed by Gustave Eiffel; the Papadis Latin is perhaps the most Parisian of the great cabarets, both exciting and romantic. We experienced the magic and charm of its elegant surroundings, striking ballets, shimmering costumes and talented dance troupes. After the show, we were taken on an illumination tour of Paris. We were shown various famous landmarks of Paris the city of lights, magically lit up. We finally returned to our hotel well past midnight. A perfect end to a beautiful evening! Our overnight stay was at hotel Forest Hill Meudon in Paris.

## Fragonard Perfume Museum

After a continental breakfast, we moved out of the hotel for a panoramic all-round view of the area surrounding the Forest Hill Meudon, and took a lot of snaps. Thereafter we visited the famous Fragonard Perfume Museum. Seized this opportunity to see and enjoy the mingled aroma of wide range of original and classic Fragonard perfumes. Prices are exorbitant we were tempted to buy. After a quick run through the entire premises we finally settled down to buy two of the classic Fragonard perfumes.

## City Tour of Paris

Our local guide for the day was a middle aged Frenchman, stocky built, jovial by nature, affluent in English with a nasal French accent, rather humorous, verbose and florid. His narrations included the historic background and a few of the little known facts of the prized monuments and the distinguished places of his beloved land. This characteristic I noticed in many of the French people I meet and admire their warmhearted friendly approach to people. Our guide, after introducing himself quickly ran through the names of the places we were to visit that day. His brief talk commenced with the series of monuments we were to see, begins with the Louvre and continues through the Champs-Elysees and the Arc de Triumph and others. The names of the places he mentioned were many and his talks were prolonged to the business district dominated by a square-shaped triumphal of its own urban area. At the end of his two days association with us he was kind enough to hand over to each of us, a booklet containing some essential details of the places to visit in Paris

We had visited the Invalides Museum. This is now the burial place for many great French soldiers, including Napoleon. Then there is the Pantheon Church, where many of the illustrious man and women of France lie buried. According to him the former prison had held some prominent members before their deaths during the French Revolution. Another symbol of the Revolution is the two statue of Liberty. One located on the River Seine and in the Luxembourg Garden. A larger version of the statues was sent as a gift from France to America in 1886 and now stands in New York City's harbor.

I shall Endeavour to recapitulate some of the grandeur and the historic importance of the monuments and places of interest our guide had familiarize us with.

## Place Charles de Gaulle

The Place Charles de Gaulle is uniquely designed. This place symbolizes the binding centre of France that President Charles de Gaulle was trying to consolidate the war ravaged France after the end of the Second World War. It is true Charles de Gaulle was unable to hold on to most of the colonial wealth of France spread across the length and breadth of the world, but he had skillfully consolidated the political, administrative, economic and the military standing of modern France. Place Charles de Gaulle is therefore a symbol of all his successes in life. It is the hub centre of many a splendor that is Paris and the glorifying past of France that France was between 17th and 20th centuries. I shall endeavor to pen the history that binds the splendor of some of the architectural grandeur of Paris that attracts people from all over the world. The Champs Eyesees is I centrally located in the middle of the Place Charles de Gaulle. At this place, is a circular square from where twelve streets emanates. Each street is named after a French military leader. Champs-Eyesees is a 17th-century garden-promenade-turned-avenue connecting Place de la Concorde and Arc de Triumphs. It is one of the many tourist attractions as there are many streets in this area which are exclusively for shopping. There are many prominent structures in this area of which Palace de la Concorde and Place Charles de Gaulle are the two among other building are worth a visit. The streets here are endowed with beautiful gardens with fountains and grand buildings including the residence of the French Presidents since 1873.

## Arc de Triumphs

Our city tour had commenced at the Napoleon's Triumphal Arch. To commemorate his victories Napoleon had commissioned the Arc de Triumphs in 1806. Unfortunately, long before the completion of this magnificent structure he was exiled and the structure was completed during the reign of Louis-Philippe in 1836. The Arc de Triumphs is engraved with names of the generals who had commanded during Napoleon's regime. The arch not only a magnificent structure but is adorned with reliefs commemorating many of the battles Napoleon had won. To name a few are the victory over the Turks and Austrians. At the top of the arch are many shields with the name of one of Napoleon's successful battles.

Arc Old Buildings de Triumphs with its many reliefs

## Champs-Eyesees

The next place our French guide had vociferously explained was the Champs-Elysées, often called Elysian Fields in English, and has a long history. In Greek mythology 'Eluia' is a place where heroes come to relax. The Avenue Champs-Elysées is probably the most famous avenue in the world. This place is used for all the major celebrations of Paris. This is where Parisians celebrate New Year's Eve and where the military parades are held on the 14th of July. At this place apart from the major historical events, many of other national events, like the Liberation at the end of the Second World War or the victory in the World Cup football were also celebrated on this wide avenue.

## Place de la Concorde

At the foot of the Champs-Élysées is built the Place Louis XV. The octagonal Place de la Concorde is the largest square in Paris. Our French guide almost wept while narrating the heartless massacre of the 1119 hapless members of the royal family who were beheaded by guillotine at this site during the French Revolution. He mentioned about the Egyptian gift, the ancient Cleopatra's Needle to Paris, is now the oldest monument at Place de la Concorde and stands witness to the inhuman deeds of the revolting mass in their frenzy to demand justice for the common man and their demand of a fair distribution of national wealth for the benefit of the common people. On this place, on either side of the Rue Royale, there are two identical stone buildings: The eastern one houses the French Naval Ministry, the western the luxurious Hotel de Carillon. Nearby Place Vandina is famous for its fashionable and deluxe Hotel Ritz and the fashionable jewel traders in the vicinity. Many famous fashion designers have had their salons located here. Indian film actor Aishwariya Rai Bachchan frequents one of those fashion salons. Our guide had talked in detail about the large statue of King Louis XV erected after his recovery from a serious illness. We were told that the square surrounding the statue was created later in 1772 and was named the Place Louis XV, but during the French revolution, the statue of Louis XV was removed. A guillotine was placed there and renamed Place de la

Revolution. Some years later its name of this place was reverted to Place de la Concorde.

## Cleopatra's Needle

Cordial relationship between France and Egypt is a long standing relationship, starting from the days of Carthaginian commander Hannibal in the prehistoric days to the time of construction of the Suez Canal by a French engineer. To commemorate those events and the long standing cordial relations with France, the Egyptian Ambassador had gifted to France the 3200 years old obelisk One of those three erected is a 23 meters tall monolith in pink granite and weighs approximately 230 tons The obelisk - sometimes dubbed Cleopatra's Needle placed in the centre of the Place de la Concorde. The pictures on the pedestal describes how the obelisk was transportation to Paris and installed at the square in 1836

## Hotel Ritz at Palace Vendome

The French people have always been known for their love of food and luxurious living style. French cruise are favored by every tourist to this Paris. The Hotel Ritz is a grand palatial hotel near Place de la Concorde at Place Vendome. It overlooks the octagonal border of the Place Vendome. The hotel is one among the most prestigious and a luxurious hotel in Paris, which today has 159 well furnished rooms and ranks highly preferred, and is one of the best hotels in the world. Ritz Hotel was founded by the Swiss hotelier, Cesar Ritz in 1898.

Paris' culinary reputation has its base in the diverse origins of its inhabitants. In its beginnings, it owed much to the 19th-century organization of a railway system that had Paris as a centre, making the capital a focal point for immigration from France's many different regions and gastronomically different cultures. This reputation continues through today in a cultural diversity that has since spread to a worldwide level thanks to Paris' continued reputation for culinary finesse and further immigration from increasingly distant climes. Hotels were another result of widespread travel and tourism, especially Paris' late-19th-centuryWorld's Fairs. At the end of the day we finally checked into Hotel Ritz Hotel or Hotel Forest Hill Meudon for a well deserved sleep before the next days' outings. Within a very short time, these hotels earned the reputation for its luxurious apartments. Visitors to The Hotel Ritz and the clients to this place included royalty, politicians, writers, film stars and singers of repute. Several of its suites are named in honor of famous guests like Ernest Hemingway who lived at the hotel for years. One of the bars of the hotel is named after him and is devoted to him and named Bar Hemingway, alongside lies L'Espadon, which is a world-renowned restaurant, attracting aspiring chefs from all over the world. The grandest suite of the hotel, called the Imperial, has been listed by the French government as a national monument in its own right.

During the Second World War, the hotel was taken over by the occupying Germans as their local headquarters. In 1979, after the death of Ritz's son; who was the last members of the Ritz family to own the place, this hotel was sold to the Egyptian Businessman Mohammed Al-Fayed. In August 1997, Diana Princess of Wales and Al-Fayed's son, Dodi, dined in the hotel's Imperial Suite before their fatal car crash

Cleopatra's Needle

## Cultural Centers

Paris has been the cultural hub centre of the world since ages, and boasts of many places of cultural excellence. The largest Opera houses of Paris are the 19th century old Garnier Opera and modern Opera Bastille Opera Bastille. While the former exhibits the more classic ballets and operas, the latter provides a mixture of classic and modern moms which are preferred by the younger generations of today. By the middle of 19th century, two other competing opera houses, namely Opera- Cacique and Theatre de la Ville came into prominence. Those were more traditionally built and occupy a large place in Parisian culture. This trend still holds true till today. Many of most popular actors of those opera houses today are also stars of French television. Some Parisian theatres have doubled as concert halls. Many of France's greatest musical legends found their fame in Parisian concert halls.

## Versailles

The magnificent Palace of Versailles with its sprawling garden was the pride of the Sun King... The Palace with its magnificent garden had become a model construction for the palaces in medieval Europe. In the 11th to the 13th century, Versailles was a prosperous village with a castle and the church of Saint-Julian. In the course time due to wars, religious rifts and military skirmishes the place was reduced to only a handful of people lived there. In the 16th century again gained importance when King Louis XIII purchased the land and built a stone lodge in 1622. Ten years later the lodge was expanded by purchasing more land. After the death of Louis XIII, Louis XIV began restructuring Versailles as a strikingly beautiful Palace with elaborately laid out garden. People say that the reason for shifting was because the Sun King distrusted the Parisians and wanted to move his Royal Residence away from the Louvre Palace, as he did not feel safe to live there due to the political turbulence...

During the French Revolution, most of the paintings and other works of art at Versailles were transferred to Louvre and the National Library and Conservatory of Arts and Crafts. After the Revolution, Napoleon spent his summers at Versailles until he abdicated. In later years the Versailles Palace was made into a grand museum, dedicated to be the glorious periods of France. I was told that a famous curator, in the year of 1960, was responsible for getting many of the furnishings back and restoring a number of the royal apartments.

Due to the shortage of time we had to be contended with a short visit to Versailles and could not go through much of the interior of this spectacular palace, as well most parts of its world-famous garden. However, our Frenchman guide had aptly explained the rudimentary aspects of this great place and we are thankful to him for his lucid explanations of our quarries.

## Notre Dame de Paris

The site of the Notre dame is the cradle of Paris and has always been the religious center of the city. This place was once the sacred ground of the Celts; the Romans built a temple to worship Jupiter. A Christian basilica was built in the 6th century and the last religious structure before the Notre-Dame construction started was a Romanesque church. Its construction was started in 1163. The Cathedral was to be built in the new gothic style and had to reflect Paris's status as the capital of the Kingdom France. It was the first cathedral built on a monumental scale and became the prototype for future cathedrals in France.

## Louvre

The Louvre, originally a palace but now one of the largest and most visited museums in the world, is a must-visit for anyone with a slight interest in art. Some of the museum's most famous works of art are the Mona Lisa and the Venus of Milo. Originally a royal palace and by the end of the 18th century it was made a public museum. A large part of the collection consists of European paintings and sculptures. There are rooms contain Roman, Egyptian, Greek and Oriental art. There are also sections for various objects such as clocks, furniture, china and some famous works of arts by Michelangelo like the Venus of Milo and Mona Lisa. In 1989 a glass pyramid has been constructed at the museum's main entrance by a renowned American architect who allows the sunlight to come in on the underground floor of the museum.

Louvre Museum

## Musee d'Orsay. Museum

By the end of the 19<sup>th</sup> century, in preparation for the Paris World Exposition two large railway stations were built in Paris, the Gare de Lyon and the Gare d'Orsay. Out of these two railway stations of Paris, Gare d'Orsay, this enjoyed the more prominent site along the Seine, opposite the Louis. The railway station had a hall measuring 175 meter long, to bring electric trains right into the heart of Paris.12000 ton metal was used for the construction of this railway station, which is more than the amount of metal used for the Eiffel Tower and was considered a masterpiece of industrial architecture. But 1939 the Gare d'Orsay platform could not accommodate for the now much longer trains. Therefore the Gare d'Orsay was out of use as a train station. Over the time the place was used as a parking lot, thereafter as a shooting stand, as a theatre location and was used even as a reception center for prisoners of war.

In 1961, the completely abandoned train station was renovated and a decision was taken to use the Gare d'Orsay as a museum for 19$^{th}$ and 20$^{th}$ century art. This Museum contains paintings of many different art forms, sculptures, engravings, photos and film. The museum was inaugurated by the French president, François Mitterrand. At the time if it's opening, the museum contained some 2300 paintings, 1500 sculptures and 1000 other objects. It contains work of painting from Degas, Rodin, Monet, Van Gogh and others.

Most of the works of art came from other museums. Over the time the collection has expanded significantly due to acquisitions and gifts. This museum mainly covers art works of all forms of the period from the mid 19$^{th}$ century up to 1914.

## Place Royal (Place des Vosges)

Napoleon in his wisdom had changed the name of the square called Place Royale to its present name Place des Vosges, to stress the importance of Vosges department, which is the first department in France to pay taxes. Later, in 1815 the same place was renamed Place Royale, Again in 1870 changed yet again back to Place des Vosges. Many famous Frenchmen lived here at this square, among them Richelieu and Victor Hugo. The Prime Minister of France lived here from 1615 to 1627. The author of 'The Hunchback of Notre Dame', Victor Hugo lived here at the Hotel de Rohan-Guemeenee. The house, now called Maison de Victor Hugo' is turned into a museum. It is hear that Hugo wrote most of his book Les Miserable.

## Hotel des Invalidely

The complex known as the Hotel des Invalids was founded by the Sun King to provide accommodation for disabled and impoverished war veterans. Originally only a number of barracks were planned. The whole complex has as many as 15 courtyards. The Hotel des Invalides is now home to several museums. A large military museum is on both sides of the

Court of Honor. It covers military history from the early Middle Ages to the Second World War, and includes weapons, uniforms, maps and banners of not only of European, but also from countries like Turkey, China, Japan and India.

## The Eiffel Tower

We were standing at the base of a gigantic structure, made of 12,000 iron pieces, so uniquely designed, ultimately to build the 300 meters tall structure, named the Eiffel Tower. It was built to celebrate the victory of the French Revolution of 1789, as the entrance to the World Exhibition in 1889.The structure took more than two years to complete and the Eiffel Tower was to be dismantled soon after the world exhibition. But the Eiffel Tower still stands today.

This tall and majestic landmark, the Eiffel Tower is the ultimate place to get a Birdseye view to see from the distance, every part of the mysterious city of Paris. One can reach to the top of the tower by climbing the stairs, which is an arduous task. The less daring ones like me would prefer to reach up to the third level by an electrically operated lift built inside the structural frame of the Eiffel Tower. Each level of the tower has an all-round viewing platform around the structure, from where one can get an all-round panoramic view of the city. As you reach the third level you would get a Birdseye view of the entire city of Paris. Seeing those beautiful buildings from top of the tower, an instinctive desire arise, to visit each and every one of those many beautiful landmarks of this historic city to be able to discover the many splendors of historical value that lie within those monuments. The Eiffel Tower is probably Europe's best known landmark and Paris's most famous symbol. In case you travel to Paris and have not planning to visit this world famous structure, you will see its top from all over Paris. The Eiffel Tower sparklingly lit up by night, in fact has become the symbol of this City of Light.

Pictures from Eiffel Tower

We enjoyed an awe inspiring experience at the second level of Eiffel Tower from where a bird's eye view of the beautiful city of Paris was a breathtaking experience in itself. One could also have gone to the level three viewing stand, which is almost at the top of the tower from where I was told, looking down to the entire city of Paris is not so fascinating as from level two.

After the exhaustive sightseeing tour of some of the salient places of tourist importance at Paris, culminating to our visit to the Eiffel Tower, we were all too tired to move around on foot, so our guide had taken us around in our bus to some more of the other interesting places and buildings particularly at the central town squares, shopping areas, museums, town halls and the opera houses that existed in the central districts of this awe inspiring cultural centre of the world. A month or for that many more months of exclusive survey of this stupendous city would not be enough to gauge the true romantics of this lovely city. I am still including the photographs of a few more places we had the pleasure to visit. I am not totally familiar with their names and importance however I am placing them in this travel memoir.

Early in the morning we checked-out of our hotel with a heavy heart for having to leave behind the edifice of those precious cultural heritages of France. Thoughts lingered on the open minded, pleasant behavior of the French people; we drove to Calais to board the Eurotunnel train to Folkston, England. Our 2 hours journey from Paris to Calais was also very interesting, particularly the early morning glimpse of many of the monuments we passed in other districts of Paris. The countryside was beautiful to look at, and the ease and warmth the people we passed, as they cheerfully waved back to us a befitting farewell.

# UNITED KINGDOM

## Eurotunnel Train

Our journey by Eurotunnel Train under the English Channel was a unique experience, whereby our deluxe bus along with many other buses, loaded trucks and cars, with passengers were moved inside this spectacular tunnel train, and we moved from the seashores of France at Calais to England. The electric train was fully air-conditioned, well furnished with all essential amenities required during the 30 minutes journey across the 22 miles long tunnel. We moved around leisurely in the train, which eventually surfaced on the shores of Folkston in England.

On arrival at Folkston, Amit allowed us one hour's free time for shopping and lunch at a wayside English restaurant. Finally we continue our journey to London for the gala events awaiting us on this day and the day that follows. The charming Prince William of Wales, a soldier in making, passionately adored by his universally revered grandmother, Queen Elizabeth II of England, was to marry a commoner Miss Catherine Elizabeth Middleton on 29th of April 2011. The marriage was being solemnized at their traditional Westminster Abbey. The entire Great Britain was in a state of euphoria and people were following every event of the marriage ceremony, the royal banquets and all events connected with the legendary Royal family with pride and gusto. Due to this national event, all members of the royal family and those from the Middleton family had congregated. Notable people from the other parts of the United Kingdom, including Ireland, Scotland, Wales, etc. were also present. Foreign dignitaries from the world over and particularly the heads of states of the 54 British Common Wealth Nations were invited. The commoners from all parts of the United Kingdom were streaming to London for a possible glimpse of the admirable royal couple.

During the hour long journey to London, we missed the clear open panoramic sights we were so accustomed to seeing in the mainland of Europe. The roads here were not so broad. Either sides of the road was generally covered with unattended shrubs which gradually changed to open meadows, then we came across colonies of red topped cottages, finally the landscape changed to conspicuous buildings, and yet I was constantly reminded that I was now travelling in the land of those people who on the commencement of the Middle ages in Europe, had gradually ruled over a major portion of the world for well over a few centuries, and was instrumental in many socio-economic reforms, infrastructural developments of the regions they ruled, and had provided a better military, administrative and trading facilities far across the seas to the lands they were gradually bringing under their rule, thus bringing stability to that region.

## A Brief History of England

Before commencing Our orientation tour of London I shall briefly narrate the history of the archipelagoes of the islands across the English Channel in the north of European mainland which is commonly termed as the United Kingdom. The combined size of these islands which form the present day United Kingdom is almost the size of our present day province of Uttar Pradesh in India.

Scrambling through the history books of Britain, in the prehistoric era, the Romans had conquered Britain in 43 AD and remained under the Rome, and were named as the Province of Britannia. Roman rule over Britain lasted till the 5th century. Then came the Anglo-Saxon and the many other sects of the Germanic races if Europe who took control of what is now a part of England and parts of southern Scotland. It is said that the Old English language had come into existence since those days. Finally the Anglo-Saxon was in control over Britain with Wales and other non English speaking people that lived in the west and northern part of England. By the 10th century this region emerged as a Kingdom of England.

Since then Kingdom of England had to face many battles with the Normans and the Vikings. Some of the landmark events are like the Normans invaded and conquered England in 1066. In the years that followed, many civil wars and battles were being fought on the mainland of Europe add its repercussions, but England remained a sovereign state till Richard I made England a vassal of the holy Roman Empire in 1194. During the reign of his brother in1212 England was reduced to a tribute-paying vessel of the Holy See till the 16th century, when Henry VIII broke away from the Catholic Church. In the 18th century during the Tudor rule England prospered and was united, to be called Great Britain.

I am highlighting some facts of the early 19th century in European history which were instrumental in the rise of the United Kingdom of Britain. Napoleon, in the period between 1803 and 1815, at the pinnacle of his military might, sought to invade England across the channel. His first intention was to block England's trade across the seas. But at that time England was ruled by HRH Queen Elizabeth I, and under her, Admiral Nelson who was having a much smaller fleet of gunboats; because of his innovative naval tactics, successfully blockaded Emperor Napoleon's seaports and that of Spain along the English Channel. Then, Nelson on 21 October 1805 sought to attack and defeated the mighty Spanish armada off the coast of Spain at the Battle of Trafalgar. As a result of the battle of the combined France-Spain fleet of 37 ships, 33 were sunk by Nelson's gun-boats. The British Navy, without losing a ship from the fleet of 32 had decisively destroyed the mighty Spanish Armada. The remaining 4 ships of Spain along with their severely wounded Fleet Admiral finally managed to limp back to the shores of Spain. During the battle, Nelson was severely wounded and he had lost an eye and a leg during the battles but, without losing a single British ship. Thus 21 October 1805 associated Queen Elizabeth's name forever with what is popularly viewed as one of the greatest victory in English History.

Once again, during Queen Elizabeth I's reign, in 1815, a second crushing defeat was given by the British to Emperor Napoleon at the Battle of Waterloo in Belgium, when the combined allied troops under the British Commander, the Duke of Wellington, at the Battle of Waterloo had completely sealed the fate of Emperor Napoleon. He was stripped of his crown and exiled to St. Helena for life. English pride gradually grew to become a leading nation in the world and by the middle of the 20th century was the ruler of almost one half of the world. Envying the achievements of the British, people across the channel on the mainland sarcastically referred to the English people as those from the land of the shopkeepers.

# London

## Guided City Tour of London

On arrival we saw that London was throbbing with life. Thousands of people were on the roads but were disciplined and traffic was being well managed. Our move around was somewhat restricted and lost valuable time for a detailed sightseeing, but our local guide gave reasonable introduction to the places. Without losing much time our English lady guide accompanied us on a guided city tour to view from a distance the Royal Palace and the Tower of London, notorious for imprisoning many of the Kings, members of the royal family and other dignitaries of England for life till death. Then we moved on to the magnificent Tower Bridge, moved along the River Thames viewing the bustling activities. Saw many panoramic scenes and important structures across the river. Thereafter we moved on, at times on foot and finally to the stately Westminster Abbey, where Prince William's marriage was to be solemnized next day. We then proceeded to St. Margaret's Church, the Palace of Westminster now being used as the Houses of Parliament, saw the Big Ben, the Country Hall, Victoria Memorial, Wellington barracks and saw the Statue of Eros at the Piccadilly Circus. We moved to Hyde Park, visited Nelson's Column at Trafalgar Square, and got spectacular glimpses of Waterloo International Railway station and equally significant Postal Headquarters of England. Then we moved to the Alexander's Palace, got a glimpse of the famous St. Paul's Cathedral, The Queens Gallery entrance perch and finally moved to the Buckingham Palace. I was not particularly disturbed because of the scanty sight-seeing visit of London as I would have ample time to revisit the places of my interest later, since the two of us had decided to remain in UK for sometime after this group tour of Europe culminating two days hence at London.

At the end of the exhaustive day we check into our hotel, had a quiet dinner in an Indian Gujarati restaurant, ideally near our hotel. That night, some of the younger couples and the spirited ones took a walk on the streets and shops of Wembley which sports a fairly large Indian community. Overnight stay was at hotel Wembley Plaza in London.

Tower of London

# Ride on the London Eye

The British Airways London Eye by the river Thames was the world's tallest observation wheel at 135meters high built in1999, till surpassed by the 145meters high wheel at Singapore built in 2010. The massive London Eye swirled, we all held your breath, looked around and enjoyed the thrilling ride on one of the world's tallest Ferris wheel. We also enjoyed taking many photographs of our group members around us, as well of the magnificent views that the city of London and its periphery could offer. The bird's eye views helped me in making my future tour plans to the city of London.

Photos from the London Eye

## Madame Tussauds Wax Museum

Later, we visited Madame Tussaud's Wax Museum in London which has many branches in a number of major cities. It was founded by wax sculptor Marie Tussaud and is a major tourist attraction in London displaying wax works of historical and royal figures, film stars, sports stars and infamous murderers. It is the world's largest exhibition of wax works which has amazed and entertained people of all ages for more than 200 years. The celebrity list includes over 400 stunning, life like figures that never fail to entice the visitors.

Photos from Madame Tussauds Wax Museum

## Shree Sanatan Mandir

We finally visit the newly opened Shree Santana Mandir at Wembley, It is a traditional construction of limestone, marble and wood, with each piece carefully slotted together without using metal. The building has been built using ancient techniques based on Hindu scriptures. While interacting with devotes who are the dedicated members of the trustee, I learnt that this magnificent Hindu temple was opened in the summer of 2010, took

14 years to build, and is made entirely of limestone imported from India. It was constructed according to the scripture of the Hindu texts, so the construction contains no steel support. Its site has an area of 2.4 acres. Many of the temple's component pieces were hand carved in Gujarat – before being flown to Britain and assembled. There are 41 marble statues of deities made in India specifically for the Mandir. The interior is elaborately decorated with carvings on the pillars and walls, as well on the shrines with painted figures of deities. To portray the openness of Hinduism, some famous spiritual leaders and forms of God from other religions are featured in the carvings, including one of Mother Teresa and the Sikh Guru Nanak. The temple is 20 meters tall and was built using funds raised by the charity Shri Vallabh Nidhi.

It was heartening to see our Indian cultural and spiritual thinking being depicted in such a wonderful way by joining each one of the stone and pillar to this Temple of God without the use of any cement or metal. Starting with the laying of its foundation stone till its completion the scripts of Hindu text and slokers have been kept in mind. Hinduism goes beyond the boundaries of each and every religion of the present age, and the study of any one of the dead civilizations. This has been amply focused to the world by none other than Swami Vivekananda in his speech delivered at the Congress of Religions held at Chicago. It was here at Chicago, for the first time the learned spiritual leaders of the world appreciated the values of Hindu spiritual philosophy. Swami Vivekananda in his numerous speeches to the youths of our nation had emphasized that the nation would grow when drastic steps are taken to properly educate the people and remove the shekels of casts and poverty. He had emphasized that the youths of the nation have to be properly educated. We have to build within our-self a sense of responsibility and courageously stand up against all forms of corruption and mismanagements.

Views of Shree Santana Mandir

If Swami Vivekananva was alive, his heart obviously would sinks in shame to know that even after 65 years of our independence on15 August 1947, we Indians are still suffering, because we, till this day still remain physically, mentally and morally not strong. In the past, between the 11th and 16th centuries we had failed to stand up against the intruding horde had come to Hindustan from the North West across the Hinduhush mountains to plunder. In later years, the invading hoards from the same direction came to find a new home in the fertile plains of Indus valley and the mighty Gangatic plains of Hindustan. Then came the Europeans by sea route to trade, then to rule over the entire Indian just because of those self seeking Indians, who-so-ever they may have been, had helped the intruders gradually to enslave the people of India.

During the period of invasion of India, that is after the 12th century. Apart from the forced religious conversions, many of the lower-caste Hindu, while searching for a respectful social identity, had willingly converted themselves to other religious faiths. Mahatma Gandhi's Sevaasrams, Swami Vivekananda's Ramakrishna Missions and other nationalistic thinkers had visualized the shortcomings in India's social structure to encourage a modular casteless Hindu society. But, the teachings of Swami Vivekananda were easily forgotten and easier methods of preaching Hinduism through the propagation of Hindu philosophy, remained as its major role by most or those institutions, therefore not attracting adequate followers or funds for running the magnificent buildings of the institutions. We who have inherited a richly philosophical ism failed to abide by a simple standardized way of living like those abiding Santana Dharma; the same liberal religious pattern practiced in the Indian Armed Forces. Similarly Sikhism, an offspring of Hinduism follow simple religious code of conduct are a cohesive religious followers. At times it occurs in the minds of many, do we Indians lack integrity, courage, resilience. Or, are we as a community devoid of a sense of dignity? What is the cause of this apathy, a lack of purpose in decision making and defined direction of thinking by some of those in authority, when they face a complex situation, or is it fear of personal insecurity, that had stops them from taking bold decisive actions.

Now a question comes to my mind, has the three hundred long years of British rule over the subcontinent of India: has the British people, left a spark of content or pure resentment for the British ethos, in the minds of the people they had ruled over in this part of the world? My aim of writing this travel memoir is to learn from the people of those countries which I had travelled, as to how, they had individually and collectively, for long durations, stood up against their adversaries, finally how they were able to defeat them, so as to lead a dignified life.

Finally our trip to Europe ended with happy feelings and good wishes to all our trip members. Our final nights stay was at hotel Wembley Plaza in London, England.

## My Synopsis of the British people

I must confess that I am not a historian, but am impressed by the British people and shall willingly share some of my thoughts about that great nation. For ages past the people occupying the British Isles have had to encounter many hurdles to establish hegemony of those islands. It is still unclear to me, whether the people dwelling in the present-day United Kingdom of Britain were the offspring of the Vikings, Saxons or the Spanish tribesmen, who, for centuries past, that is, well before the birth of Jesus Christ had been invading these islands. What so ever may have been their past, but, by the 15th century they had immerged as a democratically governed nation, that too without much bloodshed, they had ruled or had created a sphere of confidence over a very large portion of the northern and as well the southern hemisphere of this world. Their dominance lasted till the middle of the 20th century. Even during the Boer war and the two great World Wars of the 20th century, the United Kingdom was at the forefront, leading the world in times of stress. Ultimately with the help and geo=political stance by other great powers like USA and USSR, it was possible to bring about stability in the war ravaged world. That was not a small achievement by a little nation of the geographical size of the United Kingdom of Britain. And they went further after the war to harmoniously grant, one after another, independence to many of her colonial powers, and continues till today to maintain cordial relationship with all the 58 members of the British Commonwealth of Nations. To go further back in history, in the 16th century, during the reign of King Henry VIII the British presence was being felt across the shores on the mainland of Europe. The country's prominence was once again noticed during the 18th and 19th centuries, when without waging any major military campaign, the British government gradually took possession of large portions of territories across the five continents of the world by deporting the imprisoned criminals and other antisocial elements to far flung North America, Australia, New Zealand, South Africa countries of the underdeveloped world. Thus the government was giving them a fair opportunity to start a new life in a new land. While clergymen and bootleggers followed the private British trading companies to seek wealth in those far-off lands. The British Crown assisted them by renting out British soldiers for the protection of the companies interest. The trading companies and as well the individual bootleggers, were clever-enough to become the trading partners of the local chieftains of the regions of interest. Gradually the British and the other European powers expanded their sphere of influence in the backward areas of the world and were bringing more and more of the local lords were given material and as well, were helped militarily to make them more dependent on the crown. Finally, with the military help, clever logistical support and shroud state-craft the British Government was able to bring many of the local lords under their suzerainty. In this game of wits, the British people proved to be cleverer than the other European nations who had followed similar tactics in other parts of the world. Gradually, Great Britain was able to include larger portions of the profit making regions of the world to their hegemony, thereby the British economy flourished and they could spearhead may major military skirmishes in order to protect the economic interests of the British people (A role model which the United States of America is now endeavors to follow under the garb of UN). Other European countries had tried but were not so successful in becoming a world power. However in 1776, a long drawn dissatisfaction of the settlers (British and other European powers) in certain parte of North America, lead to the American war of Independence, finally resulting into the formation of the United States of America. The revolt was initially initiated by the British settlers and gradually supported by the settlers of other European nations. After their Independence, the United State of America retained much of the English characteristics, including the English language. Whereas in the beginning of the 20th century countries like Canada, South Africa, Australia and New Zealand were granted autonomy, who still pays some allegiance to the British Crown I am now going to highlight some of the significant developments made by the English people in many of the backward regions of the world which they were ruling. The Britain people had built many a thousand miles of road, rail and other modern transportation systems in the regions of occupation. Their efforts towards an elaborate educational and their legal systems are still being followed in many of the developing countries. The British people had imbibed a common educational pattern in all schools, colleges and other institutions of professional studies and research work. Many of the infrastructure developments like dams, bridges, hospitals and centers of administrative controls were developed side-by-side the developments made in their own country. Whereas the top executives and professionals were from Britain but had trained effective lower administrative staff, effective police force and a dynamically trained and appropriately equipped armed forces which brought stability to the region that lasted more than 300 years, till the British people themselves promulgated their independence after the culmination of the second world war. These were the benefits that the British people gave to the common people of the occupied regions. Whereas the earlier invaders who came to only plunder or those invaders who opted to stay behind to rule and even the local lords, generally plundered and destroyed many places of worship that had existed in the land they had occupied by force. Those who had finally decided to remain behind to rule over the people, had built many fortresses, palaces and their own places of worship, but paid little heed to the aspiration of the native people, except forcefully converting a large many to their faith, so as to create a loyal workforce. Whereas, under the British crown, expeditions were sent out into the remote areas of the occupied regions to rediscover the lost and forgotten ethnically-valuable places, that lay buried for ages or lay unattended due to some superstitious reason or other. Thus the native of the land regained some degree of moral courage, which in turn bolstered their faith and self pride. As tourism and travel to these places of increased the locals also prospered economically, but the major beneficiaries were the Englishmen and the British crown, as they had been carrying away abundance of rich raw materials at cheap rates, whereas in return, the British trading companies and British crown sold expensive finished products to the native people and yet could keep the people of the underdeveloped world happy. The British crown due to an inherent quality of fairness in dealing with the local population, were respected and regarded by the large majority of the local population. Therefore there were not many major breaches in the law and order situations which the local government was unable to sort-out. Because of their reasonable degree of fair play the United Kingdom had ruled over more than half the population of the world for many hundred years. During the Second World War in which, troops from all those regions of the world which were under the British crown, had willingly participated and were instrumental in defeating the Axis Power.

Finally, the British crown, to lessen their own administrative burden in the occupied land created many hospitals, schools, dams and roadways. The other long-term developments were the railway system and many other infrastructures for the long term developments of the country. An elaborate educational systems were developed through missionary schools particularly where formal education did not exist, excepting for some of the elite-casts a at the Gurukuls and makeshift Pathsalas for the people of the lower casts or the Madrassas to bind the Muslims to a clan; whereas the very low-casts and untouchables were shunned from every door to find solace in converting to Christianity. At some of the places in India, education implied following the doctrines of a gurus who themselves ware not known to have attended any formal educational from institutions of any reckoning to broaden his thought-process, so to live a healthy life as a human species, rather than trying to convert every individual to lead a godly life. Similarly, comprehensive legal systems were developed and where possible, existing procedures were further streamlined. Eventually, more and more of the natives were allowed to study abroad. Moneyed, local Rajas or chieftains who had dared to remain independent but craved the luxuries enjoyed by the British, were drained of their riches for their fanciful luxury trips abroad.

Some of those natives who had been abroad, for higher education and other professional studies returned home with a new found zeal of patriotism, their desire for similar freedom from foreign domination filled their hearts. Many of them had dreamed many a splendid thing for their people, but lacked the functional skills and were duped by the incompetent staff. Ultimately due to their inept and defeatist upbringing they, along with their followers blamed or envied the developed nations. Some of the spirited ones took the solemn pledge to rejuvenate the self pride and dignity for their motherland but could not garner adequate support from others around him. Some of the natives educated abroad, on return, endeavored to uplift the socio-economic standard of his motherland. A few joined the British administrative machinery in his land of origin, so as to outreach available resources to the people of his land or got involved in social reforms. A few, with revolutionary ideas got involved in awakening the sleeping mass to free them from the exploitation by the foreign rulers. Some of those educated abroad decided to settle in the profit making parts of the world. The uneducated laborers followed soon to travel abroad, some of them were bought as slave labors to the far off lands occupied by the British. Likewise other European nations played the same game in their occupied territory, but were ware less successful. Ultimately the British had their administrative presence recognized by a large portion of the world. Not that the people from the isles of the Great Britain do not suffer arrogance and many other shortcomings commonly noticed in many people of the rest of the developed world, but, I still admire them for some of their character qualities which I have mentioned earlier, which we Indians, as the people of a developing nation could try and follow their footsteps perhaps, till being recognized as one of the leading power of this world.

## Return Home with Wonderful Memories

After breakfast we check out of the hotel. Our tour has ended. It was the time to say goodbye to all our friends we had made during this trip. With heavy heart most of our associates were going to the airport for catching their flight back home. I am sure all of us enjoyed the trip and are carrying back many happy memories of us and all our associations during this magnificent tour of Europe. I am sure some of them will spare a few moments to drop a line or two or perhaps phone to share a few more interesting anecdotes they had enjoyed during this tour or any other travelled. As for us, we are anxiously waiting to meet my son Abhijit, Ipsita and their son Arunav very shortly at Southampton. Thereafter, another grueling 17 days sight-seeing of England awaited us; which I should perhaps narrating in the Part II of my travel memoir so as to figure out whether the sun ever sets over the British Isles.

......... END .........